THE OIKOS PROJECT

T0353329

The Red Room in partnership with the Architecture Foundation
THE OIKOS PROJECT
in association with the Junction, Cambridge

Oikos (pronounced ee-kos) is ancient Greek for house and the root word of economy and ecology. Embracing these principles, in June 2010 we embarked on an exciting theatre project: a unique mix of public-made art, architecture and performance that explores how a new sustainable society can flourish in a world altered by climate change.

In June 2010, in a small urban playground in the heart of London, the award-winning Berlin-based architects Köbberling and Kaltwasser started to build the UK's first fully-functioning theatre made from reclaimed and recycled materials with a group of 90 volunteers.

Together they created The Jellyfish Theatre, a theatre inspired by the two newly-commissioned plays. Focusing on energy-efficiency, co-operation and human-scale construction, The Jellyfish Theatre was showcased as part of the London Festival of Architecture in July 2010 and opened to the public on 26th August 2010.

With climate change already impacting on our lives, The Red Room with the Junction, Cambridge commissioned leading playwrights, Kay Adshead and Simon Wu, to examine ways our society may adapt for survival in these two urgent and inspiring plays written specially to be performed in this unique venue.

The Jellyfish Theatre
Marlborough Playground, 11–25 Union Street, London SE1 1LB
www.oikosproject.com

The Red Room seeks to free the imagination from the status quo. We aim to create theatre, film, debates, forums, and web-based events that challenge social injustice and promote human rights. www.theredroom.org.uk

The Architecture Foundation is a non-profit agency for contemporary architecture, urbanism and culture. Through our diverse programmes we facilitate international and interdisciplinary exchange, stimulate critical engagement amongst professionals, policy makers and a broad public, and shape the quality of the built environment. www.architecturefoundation.org.uk

The Junction, Cambridge is one of the most diverse cultural venues in the UK, a vibrant centre of youth culture and registered charity. The Junction presents contemporary theatre, dance and live art, and a diverse programme of live music, clubs and comedy. www.junction.co.uk

THE OIKOS PROJECT: TWO PLAYS

Oikos by Simon Wu

Protozoa by Kay Adshead

Introduced by Topher Campbell

OBERON BOOKS
LONDON

First published in 2010 by Oberon Books Ltd
521 Caledonian Road, London N7 9RH
Tel: +44 (0) 20 7607 3637 / Fax: +44 (0) 20 7607 3629
e-mail: info@oberonbooks.com
www.oberonbooks.com

A catalogue record for this book is available from the British
Library.

ISBN: 978-1-84943-005-0

Cover image by Document.is/credited

Contents

The Red Room is committed to creating work that challenges the status quo and to presenting theatre that is truly public. It is for this reason that the two plays here were commissioned as part of a larger event called The Oikos Project. Ths Oikos Project also saw the commissioning of the UK's first fully functioning recycled theatre created by German architect team Martin Kaltwasser and Folke Kobberling called The Jellyfish Theatre.

The Oikos Project and the two plays *Oikos* and *Protozoa* are an attempt to take responsibility for creating a different future in relation to the coming threat of climate change. Ultimately through the combination of a self-build venue and writers that are prepared to ask difficult questions it is hoped that The Oikos Project will encourage others to do the same. In this way perhaps we can create a future based less on material gain and more on being in sympathy with our only planet.

Topher Campbell, August 2010

OIKOS

BY

SIMON C.K. WU

Oikos was first performed at The Jellyfish Theatre in London on 26 August 2010

For Dino

Characters

SALIL
Asian British man, 42

ASSANA
British Irish woman, 44, Salil's wife

LILY
Salil and Assana's daughter, 21

GANGA
Indian River Goddess, played by Assana and Lily

KAMALA
Asian, Salil's elder sister, 11, played by Lily

AASHIYANA
Asian, Salil's mother, 28 (Voice only)

PRAMATH
Asian, Salil's father, 30 (Voice only)

NEIGHBOUR
Asian woman, 50, Aashiyana and Pramath's neighbour
(Voice only)

(KAMALA is outside playing Ikri-Dubri, a kind of hop scotch. She throws a round stone onto a chalked matrix of squares, rectangles and triangles and parallel lines; she then nudges this stone along with her toes, hopping on one foot through three rectangles, eight triangles in two rectangular boxes and three parallel lines representing the three worlds, four oceans and three heavens. Before you can start playing the stone has to land neatly into each empty space and not on the line to another space. The player can only stand on one foot. As she plays KAMALA holds a rag doll.)

(KAMALA is playing Ikri-Dubri, behind her is a projected image of the ikri-dubri matrix.)

Enter SALIL.

(KAMALA gestures to SALIL not to say anything to disturb her and SALIL watches as KAMALA progresses through the Ikri-Dubri matrix.)

KAMALA: *(Reaching the first level of heaven and looks back.)* Three worlds, three heavens and four oceans.

(Ikri-Dubri image fades.)

SALIL: Mum's wondering where you are.

KAMALA: Tell her I'm up here.

SALIL: You tell her.

KAMALA: Are we leaving?

SALIL: She's worried.

KAMALA: About what?

SALIL: She said the river's acting weird.

KAMALA: Huh?

SALIL: I don't know, that's what she said... it tried to suck the sari she was washing out of her hands.

KAMALA: Come on Salil.

SALIL: That's what she said.

KAMALA: *(Laughing.)* The river tried to suck the sari out of her hands?

SALIL: Look at the sky.

KAMALA: I haven't finished my game.

SALIL: It's gone a weird colour.

KAMALA: Shh… I'm trying to concentrate. *(She continues her game.)*

SALIL: Mum told me to get you.

KAMALA: Alright, alright.

SALIL: *(Looking out at the river.)* River's gone a weird colour too… look.

KAMALA: Shh, you're putting me off.

SALIL: Looks like blood.

KAMALA: *(Playing.)* Mud, not blood… idiot!

SALIL: Look at you with that stupid doll… you're the idiot.

KAMALA: Drop dead.

SALIL: You drop dead.

KAMALA: Anyway, she's not a doll, she's my lucky star.

(Salil snatches doll from her.)

Hey!

(Kamala loses the balance and falls down. Exasperated.) Look what you've done *(Snatches the doll back from him.)* and I'd already passed the three worlds and the four oceans… I was in the first Heaven, only two more to go!

SALIL: Alright, alright.

KAMALA: Idiot!

SALIL: Let's have a go, Sis.

KAMALA: No!

SALIL: Please.

KAMALA: Forget it… boys have very bad balance.

SALIL: Who says?

KAMALA: It's a fact.

SALIL: Bet I can beat you.

KAMALA: Thought you hated ikri-dubri.

SALIL: Scared I'll beat you?

KAMALA: You don't even know how to play.

SALIL: I know better than you.

(He snatches the pebble from her, shoves her out of the way and throws the pebble and starts hopping on one foot.)

KAMALA: You don't know anything!

SALIL: Yes I do.

KAMALA: So what are the three worlds?

SALIL: The three worlds are the three worlds.

KAMALA: Earth world, Inner World and the World of Siva.

SALIL: I know. *(Making it up as he goes along.)* See… easy…

KAMALA: *(Poking her tongue out at Salil.)* Urgh!

(SALIL carries on regardless.)

SALIL: I'm now in the Four Oceans.

KAMALA: Which one?

SALIL: Indian.

KAMALA: *(Making distracting noises and waving her arms. Salil wobbles on one foot.)* The Indian Ocean is sweeping you away.

SALIL: *(SALIL steadies himself.)* No it's not. See. *(He kicks the stone forward.)* Now I'm in Heaven... the sky... *(Sticking his arms out and running around, breaking all the rules of the game.)* I'm flying, I'm flying.

KAMALA: Hey, are you playing or not?

SALIL: *(Coming back.)* 'Course I am... *(kicking the stone then shamelessly picking it up and putting it in the second heaven.)* Look! I'm in the second Heaven where all the stars are... see, I'm shining, I'm shining.

KAMALA: That's not shining... that's cheating.

SALIL: Wait! Wait! *(Kick the stone out of the matrix.)* And the last one, our eternal home. *(Snatching up the stone.)* Winner! Winner!

KAMALA: You don't even know how to play!

SALIL: Winner!

KAMALA: Give me the stone.

SALIL: *(Running away from Kamala.)* Knew I could beat you.

KAMALA: Give it to me!

SALIL: *(Waving it at her.)* Come and get it.

KAMALA: You cheated.

SALIL: Beat you, beat you.

KAMALA: Start again and do it properly.

SALIL: What for? I won!

KAMALA: I'll teach you to play properly.

(SALIL snatches the doll from her and holds it out to her, but when she tries to snatch it back, he runs away with it.)

Give it back... *(hysterically.)* Salil... come back.

SALIL: Here.

(He stops, waves the doll at her but when she advances towards it, he runs away with it again. Suddenly SALIL freezes, he is staring at the river. KAMALA takes advantage of this and snatches back her doll.)

(Hushed, frightened tone.) Look at the river.

AASHIYANA: *(Voice off. Calling. Urgent.)* Salil... Salil, Kamala!

(Lightning followed by thunder.)

SALIL: *(Spell broken.)* Run, Sis, Run.

(He runs off.)

KAMALA: *(Running after him.)* Salil, wait for me... wait!

SALIL continues running and then slows down, slowing metamorphosing into the adult SALIL.

Enter ASSANA.

ASSANA and LILY are upstage while SALIL is downstage facing the audience.

The background of an open-plan office in a bank appears behind SALIL.

SALIL: *(Landline.)* Hi, Salil, City Bank... have you got the China Chemical term sheet? I just faxed it to you. Can you check? Okay, I'll wait...

(SALIL's mobile phone rings. He answers.)

I'm on the phone, I'll get back in a few minutes. Don't move. *(SALIL hangs up his mobile phone.)*

(Landline.) Good. Can you prepare a share transfer agreement based on it? I need it tomorrow... at eight on my desk... Yes, eight... No! How many times do I need to tell you... we're signing at nine! ... I don't know what they've told you... the presidents of both companies are flying half way round the world to sign this agreement? You can explain to them... good, good, good. *(He hangs up.)* Asshole!

(He dials a new number.) Where's the due diligence report? … No excuses, time's tight, we need to raise four and a half million pounds, so no fuck ups, is that clear? I don't care if you work all night, I want that report by noon tomorrow, clear? Stop muttering… can you speak like a human being, yes or no?… good! *(He hangs up and then he picks up the phone again. To his P.A.)* Can you come in please?

(SALIL talks to the audience as if he were talking to his P.A.) I'm really sick of dealing with these idiots… they charge big fat fees and do nothing… anyway, no worries, I'll fix it.

Can you work overtime… till about nine?… Thanks. I can drive you home, weather forecast's not too good… might be a downpour… don't want you getting those pretty clothes wet, do we? Are you going to the post-listing party tomorrow?… Great. There's a boutique hotel nearby, very chic, think you'd like it.

So how are things looking?… Ah yes, the Dresden Bank reception… what's day is it?… Wednesday night?… oh no… Assana wants me to watch this Chinese play with her… okay, I'd better go to the reception… Could you come too?

(His mobile phone rings.) Sorry Assana, I'm on the phone, can I call you back? *(Ends call.)*

(ASSANA in front of a screen, showing a jewellery shop.)

ASSANA: *(On mobile phone to her husband.)* But I only wanted to – *(he cuts her off.)* *(to herself.)* … I've asked Lily and… *(trails off.)*… oh well.

(Seeing a friend.)

Hi… I didn't know you worked here… I know, we've moved… Chiswick, by the river…Yes, it's really nice down there… not the move … that was a bit of a nightmare… I'm glad that's over…

Not too bad thanks... at least she knows who I am, most of the time... though sometimes she thinks I'm her mother.

The receipt? *(Desperately rummaging in bag.)* It's here somewhere. Where the hell is it? Sorry. Is that it? No, that's the receipt for the chimney sweep, we've got chimneys that need, you know... *(finding another little piece of paper.)* Wait a minute, what's this? *(Handing over a crumpled receipt.)* Thank god for that.

Lily's fine... At UCL... STS, Science and Technology... Studies... yes... With us, though we hardly ever see her these days...

Let's see. *(She examines gold ring.)* Yes, yes, that'll fit him. It's been in the family for a long time... I'm giving it to Salil for an anniversary present... twentieth... thank you... How much is it? *(Handing over credit card.)* Thanks. *(Punching in her pin number.)* Know how I'm going to give it to him? Put it on the front seat of his car... I always do that... *(Takes credit card and puts it in bag.)*

Look, *(digging in her bag and pulling out a flyer.)* can I give you... I've got one here, hang on... ah yes. *(Handing over a flyer.)* It's our latest production, 'Yellophane'... it's about how the Chinese community is perceived as invisible, you know... it kind of follows the ups and downs of a family in Barnet... I'm not selling it very well am I?... have a look at the flyer it'll give you more details.

Off to the supermarket now, something nice for dinner, a family dinner for a change, just the three of us... *(Her mobile phone rings, she searches in her bag. Finds phone. Reads text message.)*... Oh no... I spoke too soon. *(She drops phone back in bag.)* Overtime. Okay, see you later then. Thanks. *(Phone starts ringing again. Hopelessly rummaging in her bag as she leaves.)* Come if you can won't you? Bye. *(Just as she pulls out her phone, it stops ringing.)* Typical.

(Lights off.)

(Projected onto the backdrop is a big shadow of the back of a woman; the shadow is twice the size of SALIL; some Indian music playing from the radio. The shadow is moving around, busy preparing dinner. SALIL is following the shadow.)

SALIL: My mum never stopped… I followed her golden saris and her dark flesh midriff all over the place… Look, she's cooking, rolling nan with a wood belan… What're you cooking, mum?

AASHIYANA: Something Salil likes.

(Other big shadows appear.)

SALIL: People are always dropping in… patting my head, saying how big I've grown… they always want to borrow something… then they start getting noisy, chatting and laughing… My mum used to say, if you live in the river you should make friends with the crocodile and in our neighbourhood, there are quite a few round.

NEIGHBOUR: Look at his round big black eyes… he's a clever boy.

SALIL: What have big eyes got to do with being clever?

AASHIYANA: Salil, pass me my kadai.

SALIL: When my mum starts frying… the smell of ghee, cumin, garlic makes me so hungry… our little hut is steaming with people's sweat…lit with dangling wires like worms with electricity stolen from our richer neighbours, mosquitoes constantly buzzing… rats chasing cats, pungent dark smell from the sewer… life was hard but then I had my parents and the most delicious food on earth.

AASHIYANA: God is in the seasoning.

SALIL: She always says that.

AASHIYANA: Put the masala dani and katori on the table.

SALIL: *(Smelling the dish as he carries it.)* It smells… mmmmm.

AASHIYANA: *(Passing him yet more dishes.)* And the dal, baingan, mehti and your favourite, aloo gobi...

SALIL: *(Dreamily.)* Cauliflower, I love cauliflower.

(Sound of a door opening and the shadow of a large, pot bellied man appears.)

Whenever dad comes home it's time for dinner... dad's a builder and he comes home all sweaty with dust on his big belly and a dirty old towel over his shoulder... when he sees me, he lifts me up and puts my legs round his neck... Wow. Look Mummy... I'm flying.

PRAMATH: Work hard boy, then you can fly.

SALIL: He takes his hands away... I topple over, grab his neck and don't let go... he tries to shake me off but I hang on... wow... it's fun.

AASHIYANA: Put him down husband and let him wash his hands.

SALIL: He puts me down... *(slight pause.)* and he winks at me.

(Back projection changes.)

ASSANA: *(On her mobile phone.)* Sorry sweetheart, couldn't find my phone... Are you coming home for dinner?... Oh yes, sorry, I'd forgotten... Don't be too late, will you, the weather's supposed to be turning nasty and I'm not too keen on that subway late at night and the sensor light over the bridge isn't working.

(Light on Lily in front of a screen, showing the university campus.)

LILY: *(To Eugene.)* Jesus, she makes it sound like we've moved to Baghdad, it's Chiswick for Christ's sake, nappy valley... *(Imitating her mother.)* 'I'm not too keen on that subway late at night'... the bogeyman might be waiting for you.' *(She pulls a face and blows a raspberry.)*. Why pick on me?

Still texting? Like your cover... is it crocodile skin? Let's have a feel?... Come on Eugene what you doing, telling him your life history? Is he the one you met on Gaydar? Got a piccy? Let's have a look... *(Looking at image on Eugene's iphone.)* Wow, he's crossing his arms and squeezing to make them stick out, I know that trick...

Him? Huh, don't remind me... it was all going so well until I happened to notice he'd left his profile on the dating site, so I logged in with a different name, chatted him up and guess what the sweet little man did?... sent me photos showing bits of him even I hadn't seen... He was too young anyway, I prefer older men any day, at least they can talk... why are there so many juvenile fuck-wits floating around?... is that all they want - a screw? What's happened to love?

Lights off.

Excited laughter in the dark.

Lights on.

(SALIL and KAMALA on the train; PRAMATH and AASHIYANA appear as giant shadows.)

SALIL: We were waiting to catch a train, there was this gangling boy standing near me, tearing the wings off this tiny little fly, and when he finished that he started on the legs, one by one until there was nothing left but a tiny dot which he stuck in a crack in the platform... I don't want to be that fly... I'd rather be the boy...

Dad, how long before we leave?

PRAMATH: People are still getting on.

SALIL: Look, dad... there's a mango seller.

AASHIYANA: He's too far away.

SALIL: Shall we have some mangoes?

KAMALA: Can we?

AASHIYANA: Not you as well.

KAMALA: It's so hot in here.

AASHIYANA: What are you doing?!

SALIL: Dad climbs out through the train window… I defend his seat… I see him walking over the tracks… climbing up to another platform… he is struggling… the sun is shining on his back and I can see his shadow… I can never forget this shadow… before too long he is back with four fat mangoes wrapped in his shirt… my mouth is like dust, all I can think of is sinking my teeth into a fat, juicy mango… he's sweating rivers.

AASHIYANA: Look what you've made your father do… *(handing him a handkerchief.)*

PRAMATH: *(Mopping his brow with the handkerchief.)* I got the best ones.

SALIL: I want that one.

KAMALA: No that's mine.

SALIL: I saw it first.

KAMALA: Mine.

SALIL: Mum… sis stole my mango.

AASHIYANA: Kamala, you're older than Salil… you should know better… now be a good girl.

KAMALA: Not fair.

SALIL: She sulked for a few minutes but soon everything was forgotten… Kamala, what do you want to be when you grow up?

KAMALA: A doctor and save thousands of people's lives… and how about you, Salil?

SALIL: I don't know… I want to fly.

KAMALA: I want to fly too.

SALIL: But I don't want to be caught... I saw a boy on the platform... never mind... and then we stuck our heads out the train window feeling the wind on our face as the train clickety-clacked away faster... faster... faster.

KAMALA: *(Excitedly.)* The wind's flattening my nose.

SALIL: Faster... faster... faster... Sis... I'm flying... I'm flying.

(University campus projection.)

LILY: Davido?... Yeah, he's cute enough I suppose, but he's the same age as me... women mature much earlier than men, a bloke in his early twenties has the IQ and EQ of a ten year old, I don't want to babysit... yeah I'll go to his birthday party... not for him though... who knows, I might meet someone more mature there. *(Looking up.)* Jesus, look at the sky... what a weird colour, kind of purple khaki...freaky... and it feels kind of heavy, doesn't it...bet it's going to piss down with rain... Course I'm still going...who knows, love could be waiting for little Lily there... March on Eugene... come on, soldiers of love...

(Backdrop of projected image of the Ganges.)

SALIL: Ganges... sacred Ganges...

LILY: *(Marching.)*... one, two, one two three four... *(Starts raining.)* Shit, it's started... *(Running off.)* Come on!

(As SALIL speaks a BBC radio announcement fades in, mumbling away in the background, barely audible. It continues through his dialogue with GANGA and trails off when they have finished.)

RADIO: This is a severe weather warning for central and eastern parts of the United Kingdom. A storm system is causing bands of unusually heavy and persistent rain... combined with high tides there is an increased risk of flooding along the east and south coast of England. The Environmental Agency and Met Office have issued a warning of possible river flooding including sections of the

Thames. For further information phone Floodline at 0845 988 1188, I repeat 0845 988 1188.

SALIL: River Ganges… every day we bathed in her, washed our clothes, our pots and pans in her, drank, played, worshipped, lit funeral pyres… she was everything to me… everything… the mighty force born of the Holy Hindu Trinity: Braham the Creator, Vishnu the Preserver and Siva the Destroyer. Siva plays his healing music and Vishnu, overcome by Siva's music, starts to melt, Brahma scoops up the liquid Vishnu and pours him in his water pot and Ganga is born; Ganga, *(spitefully.)* the sacred river.

(GANGA appears in two forms in the screen. SALIL tries to turn his back on both her manifestations.)

GANGA 1: I can see you.

(GANGA runs around to face him but he turns away from her again but the second GANGA pops up before him.)

GANGA 2: *(Playfully.)* What, are we playing hide and seek?

(He turns his back on her but the other GANGA pops up before him.)

GANGA 1: Salil… come on, look at me… what's wrong?

GANGA 2: Don't you love me anymore?

GANGA 1: I'm your Mother.

GANGA 2: I'm your naughty little sister.

SALIL: Why did you do that?

GANGA 1: *(Echoing.)* Because.

Ganga 2: *(Echoing.)* Because

Ganga: *(Together.)* I am Ganga.

GANGA 1: Our feelings overflow.

GANGA 2: Overflow.

GANGA 1: Through cities and fields.

GANGA 2: Through houses.

SALIL: Leave me alone!

GANGA 1: I am Ganga.

GANGA 2: I am Ganga.

BOTH: Ganga.

SALIL: Leave me alone!

(Blackout.)

Enter SALIL.

Late at night. SALIL is anxiously looking out of the window at the rain.

The phone rings. SALIL hurries to the phone but is too late. He puts the phone down. Assana appears from the bedroom.

Enter ASSANA.

ASSANA: Was it her?

SALIL: They rang off.

ASSANA: Why?

SALIL: *(Checking phone.)* Number withheld.

ASSANA: What's going on?

SALIL: Phone her.

ASSANA: Just did, I couldn't get through. 'The number you've dialled cannot be reached'.

SALIL: *(Dialling Lily's number.)* Where did she go?

ASSANA: A friend's birthday party.

(He listens.)

Anything?

SALIL: *(Putting phone down.)* Same.

ASSANA: Why doesn't she call?

SALIL: She might be in the tube.

ASSANA: At two in the morning?

SALIL: I don't know.

ASSANA: *(Looking out of window and muttering to herself.)* I don't think she even took an umbrella.

SALIL: *(Looking over Assana's shoulder staring out at the rain.)* They said it would rain.

ASSANA: Rain?... it's a deluge... more like a monsoon.

SALIL: It'll pass.

ASSANA: I wish she was here.

SALIL: Maybe she's decided to stay over at a friend's.

ASSANA: She should ring, it isn't fair, she'll know how worried I'll be. Listen. Thunder.

SALIL: Staring out of the window isn't going to help, come on… don't worry, go to bed… I'll wait for her.

ASSANA: *(Still peering out of window.)* It's so dark… you can't even see the street light… it's eerie.

SALIL: Come away, come on.

ASSANA: You can smell the rain, even in here… like mud.

SALIL: I can't smell anything.

ASSANA: I don't like it.

SALIL: You're winding yourself up.

ASSANA: Listen to it.

SALIL: Well at least we know the roof doesn't leak.

ASSANA: *(Turning away from window.)* Who cares about the roof, I just want Lily to come home!

SALIL: You should have told her to be back earlier.

ASSANA: Do you think she'd listen to me?

SALIL: I know you want to give her the freedom you never had… but it's a different world, it's dangerous.

ASSANA: I told her to be careful, I always do.

SALIL: You let her do whatever she wants.

ASSANA: She thinks I fuss her enough as it is! She's an adult now Salil.

SALIL: She needs a firm hand.

ASSANA: It would help if you were around a bit more.

SALIL: And where d'you think I am, out having fun?

ASSANA: You're never in before ten.

SALIL: You think I want to stay at work that long? Things aren't back to normal yet, it's still touch and go… just to keep what you've got you have to let them think you're indispensable, without you the whole thing would go pear shaped.

ASSANA: But you're only human.

SALIL: It's not about being human Assana, it's about making profit.

ASSANA: Something's happened to her.

SALIL: Nothing's happened.

ASSANA: I can feel it.

SALIL: Don't work yourself up. Where did she go?

ASSANA: A FRIEND'S BIRTHDAY PARTY!

SALIL: I know… which friend?

ASSANA: David.

SALIL: D'you know him?

ASSANA: No.

SALIL: So who is he?

ASSANA: A university friend.

SALIL: Boyfriend?

ASSANA: How do I know, she doesn't tell me anything, she comes in and goes straight to the computer and that's it.

SALIL: Do you have his phone number?

ASSANA: No.

SALIL: You should have asked her for it.

ASSANA: I phone her on her mobile.

SALIL: What's the use if you can't get through?

ASSANA: He lives in Battersea.

SALIL: Where in Battersea?

ASSANA: I don't know.

SALIL: That's useful.

ASSANA: I hope she hasn't taken an unlicensed cab.

SALIL: You should stop all that charity work with that Chinese Community Centre.

ASSANA: I love my work.

SALIL: They don't even pay you.

ASSANA: But I don't do it for the money...

SALIL: We need you more than they do.

ASSANA: I'm not giving it up, it makes me feel... wanted.

SALIL: You're wanted at home... look Assana, you don't know what it'll like. I'm up to my ears... I need your help –

ASSANA: I hate giving dinner parties, you know that.

SALIL: Who said anything about dinner parties?

ASSANA: Look, I'm perfectly happy the way I am, okay?

SALIL: Great, and in the meantime, you have absolutely no idea where our daughter is.

(The door opens and LILY bursts in.)

Enter LILY.

LILY: Jesus Christ, you should see it out there!

ASSANA: Thank god, thank god, come here.

LILY: It's PISSING down, the underpass is like a lake, I felt like an eel wriggling about down there.

ASSANA: Take off those wet things.

LILY: We're not staying are we?

SALIL: You should have phoned.

LILY: I did, didn't I?

ASSANA: Somebody called but they rang off before we reached it.

SALIL: Your mother's been very worried.

LILY: Mum, Dad, we've got to leave, seriously... seriously... before the river floods, come on, we've got to get out of here, come on, what you waiting for?... let's go.

SALIL: You'll catch cold if you stay in those clothes.

ASSANA: *(Trying to take off LILY's wet things.)* Come on, let's get this wet jacket off you.

LILY: It's up to my knees... the roads are jammed with all these cars...but they're all empty, it's spooky.

SALIL: Take off your wet things, do as your mother says.

LILY: Come on, see with your own eyes... it's the end of the world...

SALIL: *(Reprimanding.)* It's a rainstorm, there's a bit of flooding, it's normal, it'll pass.

LILY: It'll what?!

SALIL: You're dripping water all over the carpet.

LILY: In a minute that carpet's going to be swept out to sea ... this whole house is going to become an aquarium.

ASSANA: Don't say things like that Lily.

LILY: What else do you expect me to say? You're so calm... What are we... fish?

SALIL: *(Throwing a towel at her.)* Here.

LILY: Go out, see for yourself.

SALIL: I don't need to.

LILY: Okay, you don't care, mum doesn't care, fine... *(She collapses on to the sofa.)* let the whole world collapse on us.

SALIL: Hey, not in your wet clothes.

LILY: It'll be even wetter in a minute.

ASSANA: I couldn't get through to you.

LILY: I dropped my phone, I was trying to call you and it just slipped out of my hand, plop!

SALIL: Not your iphone I hope?

LILY: I was trying to phone you and tell you to get away.

SALIL: Right, well next one's a Nokia.

LILY: Did David call?

ASSANA: Someone did.

LILY: Bet it was him, creep.

ASSANA: Lily, you'll make yourself ill, now please, take off those wet things.

SALIL: Maybe he wanted to check you'd got home safely, what's wrong with that?

LILY: He should leave me alone.

ASSANA: Is he your boyfriend?

LILY: Yuk, please.

ASSANA: Well I don't know do I?

LILY: Half man half cauliflower.

ASSANA: *(Pointing to door.)* Oh my god… Salil, look.

(Water has started coming in under the door.)

LILY: Shit! *(Jumping up.)* Told you.

SALIL: Give me that.

(He takes the towel from LILY and lays it by the door where the water is coming in.)

LILY: *(Sarcastic.)* That's really going to help, isn't it?

ASSANA: We need more towels.

LILY: We need to leave.

SALIL: Go and get them.

(LILY convulses with laughter.)

LILY: You think a few towels are going to do any good?… a bunch of M and S towels against the forces of nature!

ASSANA: I'll get some.

LILY: *(Sarcastic.)*Wow, the Three Gorges Dam's got nothing on this.

ASSANA: Come on Lily, give me a hand.

(ASSANA gets some more towels.)

LILY: Okay, fine, let's all be ducks.

Exit ASSANA.

LILY: *(Holding her head.)* Oh! My head hurts.

SALIL: What have you been drinking?

LILY: I don't know, few beers and things.

SALIL: Nothing else I hope.

LILY: How about some music?

SALIL: Unplug everything... come on. Things may get wet but it's alright.

LILY: That's what you do when the ship's going down don't you? The old palm court orchestra comes out and starts sawing away.

(LILY plays some music.)

SALIL: Stop that.

LILY: Come on Daddy, let's dance... might as well, there's nothing else we can do.

SALIL: Turn that bloody thing off, will you?

(ASSANA comes back with towels.)

ASSANA: Will these be enough?

(SALIL takes the towels and puts them by the door.)

SALIL: Get some blankets.

LILY: *(Laughing.)* Blankets! Wow, that should do the trick... the mighty Thames is overflowing its banks and what do we do? Blankets.

(Water is beginning to come into the room.)

SALIL: Better start taking things upstairs.

ASSANA: What about the blankets?

LILY: *(Sarcastic.)* Yes, what about the blankets Dad?

SALIL: *(To Assana.)* Here, help me roll up the carpet.

(As ASSANA and SALIL start rolling up the carpet, LILY dials the landline phone.)

(To LILY.) Turn that thing off!

LILY: Hang on, just phoning Eugene, he'll be worried about me.

SALIL: Later.

ASSANA: Lily?

LILY: *(Ignoring SALIL.)* Eugene, can you hear me? What's that noise?… Look I'm back home now… *(aside and whispering.)* something happened, I'll tell you later… I was out of my skull… Eugene, are you listening?… Eugene… *(she looks at the phone, the line has gone dead.).*

SALIL: Unplug the TV.

LILY: *(Feeling her ears.)* Shit!

ASSANA: What?

LILY: Is my left ear bigger than my right?

ASSANA: What're you talking about?

LILY: The music sounds really loud in my left ear, is that my left ear?

ASSANA: It's exactly the same.

LILY: *(Feeling her left ear.)* It feels bigger.

(SALIL gets LILY a glass of water.)

SALIL: Drink this.

LILY: I'm wet enough as it is, aren't I?

SALIL: D'you want me to pour it over your head?

LILY: What difference would it make?

SALIL: Drink it… help sober you up.

LILY: I've had enough water for one night thanks.

(ASSANA looks out of the window.)

ASSANA: I've left something in the car. I'd better go and get it.

(She grabs car key from a drawer.)

SALIL: Leave it.

ASSANA: It's important.

SALIL: Assana… later… we need to get everything upstairs.

ASSANA: Won't be a sec.

(ASSANA climbs out of window.)

Exit ASSANA.

LILY: *(Calling after her.)* Can you look for my iphone while you're out there Mummy?

(SALIL tries to move the rolled up carpet. LILY jogs about singing.)

SALIL: Turn that bloody thing off.

(SALIL angrily unplugs the CD player.)

LILY: It's yours and Mum's anniversary tomorrow, isn't it?

SALIL: *(Handing her the CD player.)* Now take that upstairs.

LILY: Bet Mum's gone to get your present.

SALIL: And try not to drop it!

LILY: She always puts it on the front seat of your car… be prepared to look surprised.

(A wrapped present is hurled at SALIL through the window.)

SALIL: Hey… what's going on?

LILY: Your present by the look of it.

SALIL: *(Calling.)* Assana!

LILY: Open it.

(SALIL opens present.)

What is it?

SALIL: A ring.

LILY: Bingo!

SALIL: *(Shouting out to Assana.)* Thanks, darling… now come in, will you?!

Enter ASSANA.

(ASSANA climbs back through the window, she is very wet.)

You're drenched, look at you!

ASSANA: *(Holding up a large, hooped earring.)* What's this?

SALIL: What?

LILY: Let's have a look. *(Inspecting earring.)* Is it one of mine?

ASSANA: You don't wear hooped earrings.

LILY: Maybe I should.

SALIL: *(Putting the present in his trousers.)* I'll get you a towel.

ASSANA: A hooped earring in your car… how did it come off?

SALIL: Could be anyone's.

LILY: It's really retro. *(She puts on earring.)* How do I look?

ASSANA: We've just moved… a new home, new life and now…

SALIL: *(Lugging carpet.)* We need to get the carpet upstairs… it's silk… eighteenth century… it'll get ruined.

ASSANA: *(Ignores him.)* City boy, that's what you've become?... just like the rest of them.

SALIL: Lily, will you please unplug the sodding TV!

ASSANA: An earring!

SALIL: Yes, it's an earring Assana, not a used condom.

ASSANA: Don't be disgusting. It's your secretary's.

SALIL: And if it belongs to my secretary, there may be a very simple explanation.

ASSANA: You screwed her in the car.

LILY: Ignore me, that's fine, I'm not here... didn't hear a thing.

SALIL: She travels with me sometimes.

LILY: *(Feeling ears.)* Are you sure my ears are the same size?

ASSANA: She seemed quite nice the first time I met her, I chatted to her about the move and things, and all the time...

LILY: *(Picking up the sound system.)* Where shall I put this?

SALIL: Upstairs, in the guest bedroom.

Exit LILY.

ASSANA: I've smelt her on you.

SALIL: Assana, please, not now... we've got water pouring into the front room, in case you hadn't noticed.

Enter LILY.

LILY: *(Rushing downstairs.)* Shit, look, it's really coming in.

SALIL: Do you know how much I paid for this?

(SALIL is talking while taking the carpet up.)

ASSANA: We should leave.

LILY: Yeah, let's go... come on.

SALIL: *(Holding one end of carpet.)* Lily, take that end.

LILY: I thought we were leaving?

SALIL: Do as I say.

(LILY holds the other end of carpet.)

ASSANA: Lily, pack your things.

LILY: What things?

ASSANA: Never mind, let's go.

LILY: *(Putting carpet down.)* Okay.

SALIL: Pick it up.

LILY: I thought we were...

SALIL: Pick it up!

ASSANA: We're leaving.

LILY: Come on Dad... while we still can.

SALIL: It's going to be okay, we just have to move everything upstairs and wait for it to go down again.

ASSANA: Do you think we can still drive?

LILY: Roads are all blocked Mum.

SALIL: *(Dragging carpet single-handedly upstairs.)* This is our home, we're not running away from a bit of heavy rain.

ASSANA: This is more than just a bit of heavy rain... go out and see.

SALIL: It floods in this area sometimes, down on the tow path, it's just a bit higher tonight that's all.

LILY: Talk talk talk talk talk... glug glug glug glug glug... can't we just do something!

SALIL: Your grandmother's chairs, better start taking them up or they'll be ruined.

LILY: For fuck's sake dad!

SALIL: Now!

(LILY picks up chair.)

ASSANA: We should never have moved here.

SALIL: You love it here, we all do.

ASSANA: Too close to the river.

SALIL: Assana, this is the Thames… it's regulated, controlled.

LILY: The Thames Barrier?! Huh, might just as well melt it down and make a statue of King Canute.

SALIL: The best engineers in the world built that.

LILY: Doesn't matter what they made, what anybody's made… look, see with your own eyes… it's too late, it's all too late.

SALIL: Rubbish, this isn't a third world country, there's proper infrastructure here, services, contingency plans…

ASSANA: You're so stubborn.

LILY: Well, the water's more stubborn than you, more stubborn than any of us.

ASSANA: Lily, put that chair down!

SALIL: No, bring it up here…

(LILY stands, frozen.)

Come on Lily, don't stand there like a rabbit caught in the headlights.

LILY: *(Leaving the chair at the landing.)* Better take my laptop up.

SALIL: *(Bringing the chair up himself.)* Get on with it then.

LILY: Okay okay.

(LILY takes her computer upstairs.)

ASSANA: Lily!

LILY: What?

ASSANA: Put it down

SALIL: Be quick.

ASSANA: We've got to leave.

LILY: *(Shrugs.)* I'm Switzerland.

Exit Lily.

(SALIL walks downstairs.)

SALIL: *(To ASSANA.)* Are you coming or going?

ASSANA: You had her in your car.

SALIL: For God's sake Assana!

ASSANA: I always know when you're lying, it's in your eyes.

SALIL: Let's talk about this when you're calmer, shall we?

ASSANA: I am calm.

SALIL: Are you?

ASSANA: Very calm!...

SALIL: Assana, the whole thing is in your head.

ASSANA: Am I too fat?

SALIL: You're not listening, are you?

ASSANA: I hardly see you these days...

SALIL: Look at this house... it's our dream home isn't it?... A Georgian house on the river... history, character... original fireplaces, sash windows, cornices, architraving...

ASSANA: I used to come to your corner shop every lunch time, find silly excuses to talk to you.

SALIL: We're going to be very happy here.

ASSANA: We were happy.

SALIL: I've worked hard for this Assana, very hard, not just for me, for us, all of us, the family.

ASSANA: We should have stayed where we were.

SALIL: What? Lewisham?

ASSANA: I grew up there.

SALIL: It's a dump.

ASSANA: All my friends are there.

SALIL: All desperate to get out.

ASSANA: They're happy where they are.

SALIL: If they had the chance you think they wouldn't move here?

ASSANA: That's so arrogant.

SALIL: It's true.

ASSANA: You just want to impress your colleagues.

SALIL: What's wrong with that?

ASSANA: It's just showing off... Look what I've got everybody!

SALIL: Don't you like them?

ASSANA: I have nothing in common with them.

SALIL: They like to go to shows, some of them.

ASSANA: The Royal Opera House, that's where they go, somewhere to be seen.

SALIL: Perhaps if you made more of an effort.

(SALIL gets on hands and knees and tries to unblock something.)

ASSANA: What're you doing?

SALIL: Trying to see if the drain's blocked... if I can unblock it maybe some of the water will drain away.

ASSANA: Is it blocked?

SALIL: Not sure… water's not going down…

ASSANA: Drainage must be full.

SALIL: *(Putting his hand in the water.)* If you got to know them a bit, you'd see they're friendly.

ASSANA: Why don't you just say what's really on your mind… you think I'm not helping your career because I don't cosy up to your bosses and their wives, right?

SALIL: Can't reach. Never mind, let's…

(SALIL is looking for something.)

ASSANA: Now what?

(He finds a stick, approaches the fuse box and flicks off the fuse switches; some lights go off, ceiling lights still on.)

What you doing?

SALIL: Turning some of the mains off… it's a safety measure.

ASSANA: Who started it? *(SALIL ignores her.)* Her or you?

SALIL: *(Taking corporate finance memorabilia commonly known as tombstones and some silver sporting trophies upstairs.)* Assana!

ASSANA: So everything is fine with us? *(SALIL has a handful of trophies he has gathered from a sideboard.)* Put them down, you look ridiculous holding all those trophies.

SALIL: Do you think it's easy working in the City… an Asian… in the City?

ASSANA: I never asked you to be a high flyer.

SALIL: I'm as good as any of them.

ASSANA: Better.

SALIL: I was the highest earning generator last year and that's why they promoted me… they call me 'Mister Fix It,' why?

Because no matter what the problem is, I can sort it out...
but instead of being proud of my achievements like most
normal wives would be, you seem to be upset.

ASSANA: Don't try to guilt me out Salil, don't even try.

SALIL: Yes, I want success, I'm sorry, it's what drives me...
makes me feel alive.

ASSANA: Go on, go on, justify yourself.

SALIL: You know you're really stubborn, like your mother...
and now she can hardly recognize you, you're all over
her... bit late, isn't it?

ASSANA: She needs me.

SALIL: Yes, well, so do I.

ASSANA: That's unfair.

SALIL: You're pushing me.

ASSANA: Can't you think of me sometimes, it's always you,
what you need, what you want.

SALIL: I bought you a new home.

ASSANA: You bought this for your own ego... to feel good,
a trophy home... with a power wife in it... any old wife
will do, doesn't matter who because you're fucking your
secretary.

SALIL: *(Grabbing ASSANA.)* You look really ugly when you talk
like that.

ASSANA: Leave me!

(ASSANA escapes. Salil freezes.)

I remember playing this computer game that Lily had...
the little man on the screen trying to keep his balance and
at the same time catching all these balls... at first it was
easy to juggle one ball and then two, I could even manage
three... then another one and another and another and

41

another and he started dropping them... but more balls kept coming, falling all over the place... do we need all these balls... do we need them... I didn't care anymore, I wasn't even trying... I couldn't move and the balls kept cascading down and when they hit the ground they burst and each time that happened a little part of me disappeared... I became lighter and lighter till I felt I was floating on water.

(Projection of ASSANA's eyes and Assana saying, "Too much water – so – water – no more – I will not allow – I forbid - can't afford - no more." She keeps repeating these words faster and faster until she finally breaks down.)

(LILY has come out of her room and is watching.)

No more... it's gone, we've lost it, everything! I want a ...

(LILY slowly walks down stairs.)

LILY: *(Interrupting.)* Mum, are you alright?

ASSANA: *(Exhausted.)* We're staying.

LILY: We've left it too late.

ASSANA: Too late... yes, way too late.

LILY: Why don't we sit on the roof and wave; we might be on TV.

SALIL: For god's sake Lily.

LILY: People could see us all over the world.

ASSANA: Your dad would like that.

(Water starts pouring in under the door and through the windows.)

LILY: Oh my god!

(Lights down.)

SALIL: Upstairs, come on, hurry! Move!

(They rush up the stairs but LILY, who is behind them, slips. SALIL and ASSANA do not see her slipping.)

SALIL: *(Turning round.)* Lily?!

ASSANA: Oh my god! She's fallen in... get her... Salil... hurry!

Spotlight on LILY dancing in the water, scenes of the party she went to appear on the screen – we see LILY dancing with friends, taking drugs, drinking alcohol and LILY making love with DAVID. LILY is dancing ecstatically until she falls down in the water. The screen shows LILY underwater, sometimes she is drowning, sometimes she is swimming under the water like a water nymph. Throughout the video, LILY keeps saying, "I'm here" and the ghostly desperation in her voice becomes more real towards the end of the video. At the end, she screams, "Daddy, I'm here".

Salil pulls her out of the water up onto the stairs.

ASSANA: *(In the dark.)* Have you got her?

(Very dim light up.)

SALIL: Yes!

ASSANA: Bring her up!

LILY: Where am I?

SALIL: It's alright... the lights have gone out.

LILY: What happened?

ASSANA: You slipped and fell in the water.

LILY: It's these shoes.

SALIL: Take them off.

LILY: I'm cold.

ASSANA: I'll get you a towel.

(ASSANA goes to the bedroom. Salil takes off his shirt and puts it around LILY.)

Exit ASSANA.

SALIL: You scared the wits out of me then.

LILY: I thought I was drowning.

SALIL: You should learn to swim.

LILY: I was scared.

SALIL: It's alright, you're okay now.

LILY: *(Referring to the mess downstairs.)* Look at it.

SALIL: You're shivering.

LILY: What if it keeps coming up?

SALIL: It won't.

LILY: What if the barrier is useless?

SALIL: We'll be okay on the top floor.

LILY: What a mess.

SALIL: The insurance will cover it.

LILY: But it's an act of god, isn't it?

SALIL: There are ways... I'll sort it out.

LILY: We don't need all that stuff anyway.

SALIL: Hang on a minute.

(SALIL hurries downstairs and into the water.)

LILY: What are you doing?

(He starts frantically looking for something.)

SALIL: It's here somewhere.

ASSANA: *(Coming out with a torch and a towel.)* What is?

SALIL: The doll.

LILY: What doll?

SALIL: My sister's.

ASSANA: *(Giving the towel to LILY.)* It's in the bedroom, isn't it?

SALIL: It should be here.

ASSANA: Are you sure?

SALIL: If anything happens to that doll!

ASSANA: *(Torch light gone out.)* Jesus.

SALIL: Have we got another torch or something?

ASSANA: Hang on I'll have a look.

LILY: Dad, come up will you?... I'm scared.

SALIL: It's in one of these drawers, I know it is.

LILY: What if the water suddenly rises again?

SALIL: I've got to find it.

LILY: Why don't you open the back door?

SALIL: What for?

LILY: Let the water flow away.

SALIL: Damn, where is the bloody thing?!

　　Enter ASSANA.

ASSANA: *(At the staircase.)* Look. *(She waves a glow stick.)*

SALIL: Is that all you could find?

LILY: Aren't they from Pink's concert?

ASSANA: Yes, and they're still glowing!

LILY: You enjoyed the concert more than me.

ASSANA: Did I?

LILY: Yelling and screaming.

ASSANA: We were both yelling and screaming.

SALIL: *(Yelling.)* Is that all you could find? !

ASSANA: And this.

(ASSANA hand-powders a torch and it lights up.)

SALIL: Throw it down.

LILY: *(Holding out bag of jelly babies.)* Want a jelly baby?

ASSANA: Where did you find those?

LILY: Upstairs.

ASSANA: Those are for your grandma.

LILY: She won't mind.

ASSANA: I'd better phone and see if she's alright… no wait, I'd better phone the police first…where's my mobile?… must have left it in the bedroom.

She goes up and into the bedroom.

LILY watches her mother go into the bedroom, puts the dry towel and SALIL's shirt on the floor and immediately goes down to the water to help his father.

The water is now nearly up to her waist.

SALIL: What're you doing? Stay there.

LILY: It's okay, I've taken my shoes off.

SALIL: Lily, no.

LILY: I want to help you find that doll.

SALIL: You've just got dry.

LILY: She must be there somewhere. .

SALIL: Careful you don't slip again.

(LILY starts looking for doll.).

I've looked there.

LILY: *(Checking drawer.)* Just checking.

SALIL: I've looked in all those drawers.

LILY: *(Checking another drawer.)* I know, I know.

SALIL: Lily go back upstairs.

LILY: *(Suddenly stops.)* I've done this before… water… dirty water rising up and I'm just standing there watching it rise up around me but I can't move.

SALIL: Are you listening?

LILY: Then I…

(She bends down and pulls up the doll.)

(Holding up the doll.) Here.

SALIL: Where was it?

LILY: Look… she's smiling

SALIL: Thank you.

(He kisses LILY.) Come on, let's go upstairs now.

(SALIL and LILY go up the stairs.)

Here *(putting a towel over LILY's shoulder.)*… don't want you catching a cold.

LILY: How about you?

SALIL: I'm okay.

(LILY laughs.)

What's so funny?

LILY: If people could see us *(Giggles.)*.

SALIL: What?

LILY: The whole of the ground floor flooded and what do we do?… get ourselves soaking wet looking for a doll.

SALIL: Right pair of loonies.

LILY: I love it. *(Taking the doll and drying her with the towel.)* Poor thing, she's soaked through... I knew I'd find her, I just knew.

SALIL: Will you look after her?

LILY: If you want me to.

SALIL: Be a good mother to her.

LILY: What's a good mother?

SALIL: You should know.

LILY: She's got a funny face hasn't she... like me... she can't swim either.

SALIL: You should learn to, the pair of you.

LILY: I can't bear having my head under water.

SALIL: You get used to it.

LILY: I panic.

SALIL: I'll teach you.

LILY: Will you?

SALIL: Actually somebody told me about a very good instructor... someone who could teach a stone to swim.

LILY: Thought you said you'd teach me?

SALIL: She's professional, do a better job.

LILY: Yeah, yeah.

SALIL: Where's your mother?

LILY: Phoning the police.

SALIL: What for?

LILY: Dad, is everything okay between you and Mum?

SALIL: Of course it is.

LILY: She got really upset earlier on, I've never seen her like that before.

SALIL: She's got the wrong end of the stick, that's all… I'll sort it out later.

LILY: Come off it Dad, who are you kidding?… it's been building up for months now, hasn't it… I could feel it…

SALIL: *(Interrupting.)* Leave it now will you Lily, I told you, I'll sort it out later.

LILY: I'm scared.

SALIL: We're alright up here… we'll be stuck for a bit but then it'll start going down and we can start clearing up.

LILY: What if it doesn't?

SALIL: It's not going to get any higher than this.

LILY: Dad, the entire weather system falling apart.

SALIL: Now you sound really British, blaming everything on the weather.

LILY: Come on, dad.

SALIL: It's just high tide and heavy rain, that's all, the rain will stop, the tide will turn and everything will be fine.

LILY: And we'll all live happily ever after.

SALIL: Thanks for finding the doll, Lily.

LILY: Now you owe me a favour.

SALIL: Anything… what do you want princess?

LILY: *(Pause.)* If I tell you something, promise you won't be angry?

SALIL: Try me.

LILY: I did something stupid.

SALIL: Go on.

LILY: No, not now.

SALIL: It's alright, tell me.

LILY: Doesn't matter, honest.

SALIL: Lily, you're making me nervous.

LILY: Sorry.

SALIL: What is it?

LILY: I can't remember.

SALIL: Something's worrying you?

LILY: Maybe.

SALIL: Don't you trust me?

LILY: Wish I hadn't said anything now.

SALIL: Come on Lily, I'm your father.

LILY: I hardly ever see you.

SALIL: Yes you do.

LILY: You couldn't even make it to my birthday.

SALIL: Hey… who bought you that ipad?

LILY: Hey… who wasn't there?

SALIL: You're lucky, I never got birthday presents, my toys were sticks and stones, anything I could find.

LILY: Does having an ipad make me lucky?

SALIL: That doll was what the only toy your aunty ever had.

LILY: She must have really loved it.

SALIL: Look, Lily… I've had to work hard, all this, everything we own has come from hard work.

LILY: Even at weekends?

SALIL: I started out in a corner shop, you know that?

LILY: You told me.

SALIL: Your mum was a waitress…

LILY: And you were both earning peanuts, I know.

SALIL: If I hadn't studied for a part-time degree in finance and got a job in a bank we'd probably…

LILY: … still be there now.

SALIL: Money doesn't just fall in your lap Lily, you have to work at it.

LILY: Oh no! Look it's coming up again.

SALIL: Come on.

(They move higher up the staircase.)

LILY: It's not going to stop, is it?… it's going to keep rising and rising.

SALIL: It's going to be alright.

LILY: *(Calling out.)* Mum?

(Coming out from the bedroom with her mobile phone glued to her ear.)

What's going on?

ASSANA: Can't get through.

LILY: What, 999?

ASSANA: Yes!

SALIL: Did you get through to the home?

ASSANA: Left a message, they're not answering either… Hello. Hello can you hear me?

LILY: Thank god, thank god!

ASSANA: Sorry? You're breaking up… just a minute…

(ASSANA walks back to the bedroom. LILY rises as if to follow her mother.)

SALIL: So tell me… who is this David?

LILY: What are you talking about him for?

SALIL: You went to his party.

LILY: So?

SALIL: So who is he?

LILY: A friend.

SALIL: Alright, if you don't want to talk about him.

LILY: I want to know if Mum's got through.

SALIL: Earlier on you seemed a bit upset, that's all, I was just wondering…

LILY: *(Interrupting.)* I don't want to talk about it.

SALIL: About what?

LILY: Everything's a mess, full stop, end of story.

SALIL: End of what story?

LILY: All this… you quarrelling with mum… the party…

SALIL: Didn't you enjoy it?

LILY: It stank.

SALIL: I know what you mean… I've been to some pretty awful parties in my time, made a complete ass of myself… spilled wine on the carpet, threw up on someone else's bathroom floor.

(Pause.)

LILY: I went with him.

SALIL: What?!

(Silence.)

I see.

Protected?

(LILY shakes her head.)

Oh dear.

LILY: And it's two weeks after my period.

SALIL: Why?

LILY: I don't know, I don't even like him that much.

SALIL: What were you thinking?

LILY: I don't know what I was thinking, I wasn't thinking.

ASSANA: *(Reappearing from the bedroom and seeing the risen water.)* Oh my god, look at it!

LILY: What did they say?!

ASSANA: I think they said something about staying put and they'd try to get us out... it was terrible reception... I could only hear one in every four words...

LILY: When?!

ASSANA: Don't know... I'm not even sure if that's what they said.

LILY: I wish they were here now.

SALIL: I think it's peaked, look, it's started going down.

LILY: Dad, we're not stupid!

ASSANA: I'll try the home again.

(ASSANA is about to go back to the bedroom.)

LILY: Don't go.

ASSANA: There's no reception here... I won't be long... I have to find out if grandma's alright.

Exit ASSANA

LILY: *(Rising up to follow her mother.)* Mum.

SALIL: It's alright Lily, let your mother try and get through.

LILY: I wish I could wake up and all this would disappear.

SALIL: Maybe you should see a doctor.

LILY: Why? You don't think I'm pregnant, do you?!

SALIL: No harm in finding out.

LILY: Shit.

SALIL: And you know… diseases.

LILY: Stop it!

SALIL: Better to be on the safe side.

LILY: Stupid, stupid!

SALIL: Why did you do it?

LILY: I don't know… the climate's fucked, my head's fucked, everything's fucked… half the time I don't know what I'm doing…I don't even know who I am anymore.

SALIL: You're young…

LILY: Don't patronize me, Dad. What's the average marriage age for girls to get pregnant in India… eighteen, nineteen? It was more like twelve or thirteen in the old days, wasn't it?

SALIL: This isn't India.

LILY: I could always become a nun, I suppose.

SALIL: A pregnant nun?

LILY: Stop making fun of me!

SALIL: I'm not.

LILY: Yes, you are, you're such a good liar, you've even managed to lie to yourself.

SALIL: Hey, come on, that's not the way to speak to your old man.

LILY: That's the problem, dad… there's no right way of speaking to you… it's been like this for a long time.

SALIL: Why are you so angry all the time?

LILY: Because Mum's right… you've done all this, not for us… but for yourself.

(LILY throws the doll at SALIL.)

SALIL: Hey! *(Picking up the doll.)* I thought you were going to be a good mother to her… she's my lucky star, *(to the doll.)* aren't you?

Enter ASSANA.

ASSANA: Just spoken to Mum, she says she likes the rain, it is washing everything clean apparently. Where are they?… they should have been here by now.

SALIL: I'm not leaving.

ASSANA: Of course you are, we all are.

SALIL: It's my home… *(shouting.)* no one's going to force me out of my own home.

ASSANA: You can come back when the water's gone down.

SALIL: High tide and a bit of rain…

LILY: A bit of rain?! Dad, half the house is underwater.

SALIL: I'm not scuttling off like a water rat.

ASSANA: Salil, we can't stay here.

LILY: We'll be drowned!

SALIL: You go. I'm staying.

ASSANA: Remember when we first met?... You said you'd look after me. We found each other and we said we'd always stay together, no matter what. If it wasn't for that promise, I wouldn't be wasting my breath.

LILY: Dad... You can't stay here, it's insane!

SALIL: No, I'm sorry but I'm not leaving and there's nothing anyone can say or do that will make me change my mind.

LILY: Look Dad, unless you suddenly grow fins and a pair of gills you don't stand a chance.

SALIL: This is our home.

LILY: They were all drowned weren't they? Your mum and dad and your sister, in Kashi when the Ganges flooded, right?... so you should know... of all people, for god's sake, you should know how fucking dangerous this is.

SALIL: They weren't drowned.

LILY: Excuse me?

SALIL: They were killed... by Ganga.

LILY: Ganga?

SALIL: Pucca houses, mud walls, thatched roofs... they were no match for her.

LILY: Her?

SALIL: This house is solid... brick walls, slate roof, cement.

LILY: And it's filling up with solid water.

SALIL: When Ganga rose up, she destroyed everything... we climbed onto the roof, but the water kept rising and the house started dissolving beneath our feet ... I was the first to jump... like a monkey into the nearest tree... and when I looked back, our house was gone ... one minute everyone was there next to me... the next, I was all on my own up a tree, water swirling round me.

ASSANA: And if your father wants something, he hangs on tooth and nail till he gets it.

SALIL: It grew dark, I wanted to sleep, to let go… then Ganga appeared.

(ASSANA and LILY appear as GANGA on the screen; they speak individually and sometimes in unison.)

GANGA 1: Look at you, clinging on to that tree like a coconut.

SALIL: Go away.

GANGA 2: That's not a very nice thing to say. What's wrong? Don't you like me anymore? I thought you loved me.

SALIL: Where's my mum and dad and my sister … where have you taken them?

GANGA 1: I am your mother.

SALIL: My real mother.

GANGA 1: Are you thirsty? *(He shakes his head.)* A boy like you stuck up a tree, you must be dying for a nice, long, cool drink.

(SALIL does not answer.)

Here, drink, drink.

SALIL: I want my mum and dad… I want my sister.

GANGA 2: I am your sister.

SALIL: My real sister!

GANGA 2: You must be bored up there in that tree, come down and play.

SALIL: Don't want to.

GANGA 2: We can play ikri-dubri, you're good at that aren't you? *(Playing.)* I pass the Earth World, Inner World and now I'm in the World of Siva.

SALIL: She's better than you... she could beat you any day!

GANGA 2: Look, I'm in heaven... your sister's in heaven... she'll soon reach the eternal home... there... I'm the winner... winner.

SALIL: Why did you do it?

GANGA 2: It's only a game.

SALIL: It's cruel.

GANGA 2: Beat you... beat you.

SALIL: You're nothing to me, nothing.

GANGA 2: Come on... don't be such a bad loser.

SALIL: Why didn't you just stay where you were!

GANGA 1: How could we?

GANGA 2: Even if we wanted to.

GANGA 1: Is the shabby little hut your home?

SALIL: I loved you... I worshiped you.

GANGA 1: That's why I'll never leave you.

SALIL: You've taken everything.

GANGA 1&2: There's more.

SALIL: Everything's gone.

GANGA 1: Look at me, Salil.

SALIL: Don't want to.

GANGA 2: Look closely...

GANGA 1&2: Look.

(Screen off.)

SALIL: Then I looked at Ganga... I looked at her hard like I'd never dared look at her before... and you know what

I saw?... I saw myself and at that moment, I knew I was completely and utterly alone. I woke up in a tent and later I was adopted by a relative who was married to an Englishman... when I first walked into their house I felt like a maharaja, it was the first time I'd seen a chandelier... then they gave me a room... my own room... first thing I did was bang on the wall with my fist... feeling how strong it was... then I knew that what killed my family was not the River Ganges, but being poor... being backward... being vulnerable... there is no Ganga... no Father Thames... (*SALIL* defiantly tips water over his head and vigorously shakes his head dry.) I am bigger than both of them... because I'm real...

ASSANA: Stay then, I don't care anymore.

LILY: You think this isn't real?... can't you see what's happening?... the barrier's no good anymore, the whole fucking river has risen up and it's going to sweep away you, me, mum, this house and everything else that gets in its way.

SALIL: It's done, decided... you two go, I stay... I'll join you later.

ASSANA: We don't even know if anyone's going to come!

LILY: What are you looking for Dad? There's no answer here.

SALIL: It happened once ...but it's not going to happen again... not here.

LILY: It's going to keep rising and rising dad... and you'll be trapped, nowhere to go.

SALIL: I jumped... I thought she was following... but they held her back, the tree wasn't strong enough for two of us.

ASSANA: Let it go Salil... that was a long time ago...

SALIL: Kamala could easily have jumped... they held her back.

ASSANA: For God's sake, Salil.

SALIL: I was the son so I jumped first and then they stopped her to save me... We murdered her... all of us... But they were the lucky ones, they died with her, they were forgiven.

ASSANA: We've got to get out of here... where are they?

SALIL: I ran as far away as I could and struggled to get to the top, so I'd be up there, high up there so no matter how high the waters rose I'd be safe... even if I lived by a river.

LILY: You think you're fighting but you're not, you're just running away... from where you came from, from what you were. I don't want a dad who keeps running away.

SALIL: Running away?

LILY: You don't fight a river... you try to understand it.

SALIL: You have no idea.

ASSANA: What if they don't come?

LILY: Shit, look... water... even here!

ASSANA: Oh my god!

LILY: What are we going to do?!

SALIL: Don't panic, it's a surge, that's all.

LILY: There's nowhere else to go?... mum... dad...

SALIL: We're going to be alright.

ASSANA: It isn't alright.

SALIL: Assana, what are you saying.

ASSANA: We have to climb on the roof.

LILY: Wait?

ASSANA: What?

LILY: Listen.

(Silence, sound of helicopter far away)

(Excited.) They're coming.

ASSANA: Thank god! Hurry! Hurry! Come on! What's keeping them?! Are we ready? Everything ready?

(Sound of helicopter getting louder and ASSANA's mobile phone at the bedroom rings. ASSANA goes to answer the phone.)

(Pause.)

SALIL: I didn't think of my sister when I jumped... I always won when we played games.

Enter ASSANA.

ASSANA: They're here! They said two at a time.

(SALIL gestures to them to go.)

LILY: Make sure you follow.

ASSANA: You'd better, there's a lot to talk about... we haven't finished yet.

Lily, come on... move.

SALIL: *(Giving her doll.)* Here. Remember... she can't swim.

LILY: But you're going to teach her... right?

SALIL: Yes, I am... see, finally everything is sorted out.

(Just as she is leaving, LILY turns back.)

LILY: You're coming too, aren't you?

SALIL: Think I'd miss a chance to fly?

(ASSANA and LILY are lifted off the stage.)

(SALIL looks around and pushes against the strong walls. Assana's phone is ringing but SALIL does not answer. He stays.)

Lights down.

Dim lights up

Rolling video projection

UK – Floods

- 2000 south-east England, the worst flood for 40 years.

- 2002, York and Pickering, more than a month's worth of rain in less than 24 hours and floods in Glasgow caused severe damage.

- 2003, more than 100 flood warnings.

- 2004, Cornwall, worst flood since 1952, 150 people airlifted to safety, millions of pounds of damage

- 2005, Cumbria, worst floods since the 1820s, more than £250 million of damage.

- 2007, The floods of 2007, 13 deaths, affected 48,461 homes, 6,896 businesses and around 850 schools.

- 2009, Cumbria, a total of more than 12 inches in 24 hours, a UK record for 24-hour rainfall.

The World – Floods

- Africa. The 2000 Mozambique flood covered much of the country for three weeks, killing thousands, leaving the country devastated

- USA. In 2001, floods killed over 30 people in the Houston, Texas, area.

- Europe. The 2002 European floods hit Central Europe, causing major damage.

- Canada. One of Canada's most devastating floods occurred in southern Alberta in 2005. 4 deaths resulted from the three-week flood.

- India. Flooding in Mumbai, India, in July 2005 left over 700 dead. Some areas were under 5 metres of water.

- USA. 80% of New Orleans, Louisiana, USA was flooded in 2005 during Hurricane Katrina when. 1,076 people died.

- Eastern Europe. Rain across Eastern Europe in 2005 caused severe flooding.

- Korea. Both North Korea and South Korea saw one of their worst floods ever in 2006.

- USA. The Mid-Atlantic States flood of 2006 in the eastern United States is the worst since the flooding caused by Hurricane David in 1979.

- Africa. Ethiopia saw one of its worst floods ever in August 2006.

- Indonesia & Malaysia. Floods hit Jakarta in 2007, killing 80 and in Malaysia the worst floods recorded in over 100 years with 100,000 people evacuated in Peninsular Malaysia, Sunatra, and Sabah.

- Australia. The 2007 Hunter Floods claimed 11 lives and forced the evacuation of 4,000 people.

- Africa. The 2007 Africa Floods were the worst in Africa's history with 14 countries affected.

- India. In 2008 floods in India killed an estimated 2,404 people.

- USA. 2009 saw the second worst flood in Manitoba in the United States since 1826 with damages in millions of dollars.

- Saudi Arabia. The 2009 Saudi Arabian floods have been described by civil defence officials as the worst in 27 years.

122 people were reported to have been killed, and more than 350 missing.

- France. In 2010 the worst flooding in south-eastern France in more than 180 years claimed 25 lives.

- China. In 2010, torrential rains hit 18 provinces, more than 1000 people reported dead, over 12 million people evacuated.

- Pakistan. In July and August 2010, flooding in northwest Pakistan killed over 1,600 people with over 15 million people affected and the worst in 80 years.

PROTOZOA

BY

KAY ADSHEAD

Protozoa was first performed at The Jellyfish Theatre in
London on 23 September 2010

Characters

There are 3 actors (4 characters)

SHEANN

Female, late teens, black or mixed race, a
Northerner.

CORDELIA

Female, 40s, white, a Southerner.

HALL

Male, 50s, a police inspector, an Asian
Londoner.

EGASHA

Female, early teens, black or mixed race.

CHORUS

Notes: The mute chorus of women changes the scene when
necessary.

They are so deft as to be almost invisible.

Throughout the play they become more visible and they
grow in number.

The film is black and white and always under or over
exposed, in long shot, or extreme close up. Ideally it is
projected into the entire space. It is silent. It represents,
illustrates and expands the world of the women.

The sound is to create panorama or intimacy. It represents,
illustrates and expands the world of Hall, Cordelia and
Sheann. It populates their world.

SCENE 1

Pitch blackness. Absolute silence.

Then –

A huge splash, – a breath, – a sudden beam from a floodlight finds a young woman, violently, breaking the surface of water. She is gasping. She is almost naked. She tries, desperately, to haul herself out but she is exhausted; half dead. Finally after many painful attempts she succeeds. She is coughing, spitting, panting.

A moment's stillness.

Then she remembers, she starts to whine, rock, she becomes distressed… she looks round. And she calls over… and over… and over…

SCENE 2

It is after the floods. A calm, English summer evening.

An emergency neighbourhood meeting has been called in a hastily put back together, public building. There is no mains electricity; lights, from various establishments, have been seconded and are in use, including what might be a football pitch floodlight.

On a makeshift platform there are seven bizarrely assorted and storm damaged chairs, six are empty. In the last sits CORDELIA STANDISH. Perhaps she is in her early 40s. Slim, striking and businesslike; in a demure, beautifully tailored suit, only mud on the shoes tells the tale of the times.

INSPECTOR HALL stands, slightly uneasy, he is not a natural public speaker.

SOUND

From another room or adjoining building, anxious echoey voices. Footsteps. Occasionally the sound of wailing and distress, people being pulled away, resisting.

HALL: So…

    it appears

rumours of
an Apocalypse
may indeed
have been
exaggerated.

He tries to smile.

But
we
are
experiencing
a total
communications
breakdown here,

certainly the
first of
my career

I can
only reassure
you

blocked roads
are being
cleared,
railway lines
repaired,

rescue zones
established.

He tries to smile again.

Power supplies
will take
a little longer

And I know
you're all
desperate

to use
mobile
phones...

Those
who still
have them,

He tries another smile.

the ladies
are anyway,

which is
a good point
to introduce

Cordelia Standish,

He gestures. She smiles, relaxed.

some of you
know
her already
as a
neighbour.

Miss Standish
has volunteered
to act
as mediator,

between
the police,

and local
residents
like yourselves
who choose
to stay
in
their property.

Pause. Sternly.

I want
to make
it
quite clear

You do
that
entirely
at your
own risk

Emergency Services,
including
Air Recovery
Operations,
are pulling out.

Another smile.

But
we aren't
going
to abandon you
completely.

At the end
of this meeting
we ask
you
to form
a queue
at the
right hand
side of
the old
playground.

Each household
will be supplied
with 3 gallons

of water
per person

a 14 day
supply of
non-perishable
food

*From the back of the room there is a flurry of noise and voices... a
scream... a gasp.*

HALL: a
electric
tin opener...

*A young woman enters. She is completely naked now. Her hands are
bleeding. She looks blankly at the gathered. She sits on one of the
seats. HALL, initially disconcerted, takes off his coat and attempts
to cover her.*

SHEANN: *(Softly, very intimately, as if speaking to someone she
knows.)*

Well,
I've just come
from the
library,

and
my daughter
i'nt there.

There
was no-one
at the front
desk

no-one
at all,

not even
that ginger
minger

with the
jumpers,

that won't
let you
eat crisps.

I went
up
the winding
staircase,

I've never
done that
before,

and there's
pictures
hanging on
the walls
in those
twiddly frames

of
really old
men,
important
men –
like off
the telly
sometimes,
with fuzzy
hair on
their face
and
watches on
chains.

I went
to the top,

and the
door was
open...

heavy
wood door
carved with
waves from
the sea

and great
smiley faced
fishes
with curly
tails

and

men in
boats

and I
went into

the room

which was
long
and dark
and dusty

with
piles of
broken books
from
floor to
ceiling

piles and piles.

And then
the moon
must have

come from
behind a
cloud,

I suppose
it did

I suppose
that's what
must have
happened,

and I
saw then

that the
room

was full
of
dead children…

SOUND

Fearful whispers.

SHEANN: and they
were
lying on
the floor

and their
eyes were
open and
staring,

and they'd
put the
little ones,
the babies,
together
in the far
corner

and I
had to
like
step through
being
really careful

Softer still.

And I'm sorry
I'm really sorry
but
I stepped
on a hand

I stepped
on a tiny
finger

I looked
and I looked

but <u>my</u>
baby,
my Sascha
wasn't there,

I'm sure
of it,

I'm sure
of it.

So

after a
while I
tip toed
back down
the staircase,

and I saw
that most

of the windows
had no
glass,

it had
shattered
and was
lying in
sparkly piles

and I

picked up
a long
sharp jagged
bit

and I
scratched out
the
eyes of
the painted
old men,

I scratched
them out.

SOUND

Whispers have turned into a frozen silence.

FILM

Flickers into... close up of feet... in sensible shoes walking along the river's edge.

There is storm debris underfoot, and all about... broken plates... hair straighteners... toys... computer bits... a trouser press... we can still see pebbles, stones.

Suddenly we see a black/mixed race baby, about nine months old, as if washed up from the river... film flickers and disappears.

During the film, two women reset the scene. We may not notice them. They are almost invisible.

SCENE 3

Morning. Bright English sunshine in what remains of CORDELIA's house. It has been destroyed in the storm and the slurry.

SHEANN, in a tracksuit now, is lying on the floor with a pile of rescued, dog-eared paper, and pens. She is drawing. Her hands have been bandaged.

CORDELIA enters, in what before the flood might have been country walking clothes. She is packing a rucksack.

CORDELIA: (*Well spoken.*)

I'm going
out

Pause. SHEANN says nothing, continues drawing.

Did you
hear me?

Slight pause.

SHEANN: (*Softly.*)

Yes.

CORDELIA: On a
recce.

I'm going
to see
for myself
what is
really happening
out there.

Pause.

She sorts through the rucksack.

I mean
honestly!
these people
are such
wimps

"ooh...
my house
has blown
down

what form
do I fill
in?"

SHEANN continues drawing, saying nothing.

Mmm.

Well I
can't say
don't answer
the door
to anyone,

because
there isn't
one.

She laughs. SHEANN continues drawing, though it is now evident she is listening intently.

From her pocket, CORDELIA takes out a lipstick. She doesn't have a mirror. She applies it "blind".

Pause.

Have you
heard a
single word
I've said?

SHEANN: Is there
    anything to
    eat?

    Pause.

CORDELIA: Eat?

SHEANN: Yes, I'm...
    I'm hungry

CORDELIA: *(Thoughtful, with some distaste.)*
    Right...
    Right...

    *She goes off, comes back with a small can of beans, which she opens
    with a tin opener. She thinks.*

    Surreptitiously, she puts the tin opener in the rucksack.

SHEANN: Thank you.

    CORDELIA makes to leave.

    I'll need
    a spoon.

CORDELIA: Right...

SHEANN: And
    water
    I'll need
    water

    Cordelia goes off, comes back with a spoon and a small water bottle.

    She looks down at SHEANN's picture... perplexed.

SHEANN: It's my daughter,
    a picture
    of my
    daughter.

    I'm going
    to draw

lots and
put them
everywhere,

all along
the river bank

CORDELIA: Don't you
have a
photograph?

SHEANN: *(Shakes her head.)*
I did
have one,

I had
one in
my purse.

She was
sitting on
a swing.

She was
laughing.

You could
see her
funny gums.

CORDELIA: *(Awkwardly.)*
Right...
I'll...

She makes to go.

SHEANN: Will you
get back
before it's
dark?

Pause.

CORDELIA: I can't
    say...

    Pause.

    Yes
    I suppose.

    Pause.

    I'll try.

    Slow moving shadows show time passing... perhaps 2 hours.

    SHEANN has made more posters.

    She stands, about to leave, when HALL arrives.

SHEANN: Oh.

HALL: *(Disconcerted. Polite.)*
    You...
    You're still
    here.

    HALL looks around.

SHEANN: She's out.

HALL: Out?

SHEANN: She's gone out.

HALL: On her
    own?

SHEANN: Yes.

    Pause. HALL looks about.

HALL: She can't
    be serious
    about staying
    here,

a woman
like her,

of her class.

He looks at SHEANN, who says nothing.

It's completely
derelict...

Where can
she sleep...
eat?

It's dangerous
Surely?

It's
unsanitary

SHEANN: She's going
to rebuild
it

HALL: How?

SHEANN: Don't ask
me,
I know
nothing
about the
woman.

HALL stops, he looks at her.

HALL: *(Softly, still politely.)*
I suppose
you think
you've fallen
on your
feet?

SHEANN: I don't
know what

you're talking
about

HALL: Invited in
    as a
    house guest
    to a rich
    businesswoman...

SHEANN: She dun't
    seem rich
    to me

HALL: ... Suddenly
    in the
    hub of
    our local
    community.

SHEANN: Where's
    the hub?

    I've been
    here 3
    days,

    you're her
    only caller.

HALL: *(Pause. Scrutinising her.)*
    Why are
    you here?

    Mm?
    Now,

    here
    particularly?

    There's lot
    of places
    for you
    to go

that would
be more...
comfortable…

Pause.

SHEANN: I lost
my baby

on the
river bank

out there

I have
to find her

HALL: Well
it's very
kind of
Miss Standish
to take
you in

offer you
food and
shelter

isn't it?

Very kind
indeed.

SHEANN: Not as
if I
can nick
owt.

HALL: I'll be
watching you

SHEANN: Will you?

HALL: Yes

He makes to go.

SHEANN: *(Deadly, determined.)*
    And I'll
    be watching
    you

    Inspector
    Hall

SCENE 4

Time passes in moving shadows. Perhaps five hours.

Night. CORDELIA's house.

CORDELIA enters, expecting to see SHEANN. She is gone. She is all alone.

She is white faced and exhausted, she sits, she is shivering.

Suddenly she starts to shake and rock, moaning like an animal.

Footsteps... CORDELIA composes herself, goes to a hidden recess, takes out a small, strong, old-looking metal box. She opens it, takes out a small old gun, she points it.

SHEANN enters, she is muddy and wet up to her knees. She has been looking for her daughter.

SHEANN: Please
    Shoot me!

    CORDELIA puts the gun away. Suddenly she is frantic.

CORDELIA: Fire...
    right?

    You need
    to dry
    off

    warm up...

    Well

Looking around.

there's a
flat bit
of ground
there look,

don't know
what it was –
kitchen table
p'raps –

Anyway,

matches…,
we need…

She heads off, leaving SHEANN shivering.

She comes back with a large box.

See –
Here we are,
Good!

She opens the matchbox, tries to strike one, … it's damp.

A bit
damp,

well

they'll
dry

She puts them down.

And we'll
need wood,

you know

logs,

they sell
them at
the...

She laughs, realising there are no shops.

Sticks!

There's
great piles
of sticks
outside
on the
river bank,

and
drift wood
of course

just inside
the front
porch

Wait!

She dashes out.

SHEANN is having difficulty breathing now, almost an asthma attack.

*CORDELIA Returns with an armful of sticks and twigs and bracken,
and a pile of rubbish.*

She tries the matches again.

No good.
Well,
we'll have
to

rub two
sticks together,
you know
like the girl guides.

She gets two from the pile, makes a nest of kindling.

Here

She hands the sticks to SHEANN.

Rub them
together

SHEANN backs off, says nothing.

Did you hear me?

Rub the
sticks
together!

SHEANN does nothing, says nothing.

CORDELIA speaks louder... miming.

RUB THEM
TOGETHER.

SHEANN: I heard
you
I'm not
doing it.

CORDELIA: Oh
for goodness
sake

CORDELIA furiously rubs the sticks into a pile of bracken and rubbish.

Getting into a rhythm.

Well...
you'll be
interested to know

there's been
a change
of plan,

apparently.

Having told
everyone to
leave the
disaster areas

pronto

without packing
so much
as a
spare pair
of pants

We are now
being told

quite firmly
as it happens

to stay put!

A Rapid Response
to threats received
against National Security

We are on
RED ALERT.

So for now
Sheann
we are
"corralled",

I think
that is
the correct
terminology...

She is still vigorously rubbing the sticks.

Well,
don't know
about you

but I'm
warming up
nicely.

Pause. She stops, softly

Everything's under
mud out there now.

And there's
mountains,
iron mountains
of stuff,

50 or 60
cars blocking
the underpass.

At the end
of the road
there's a bus
stuck in a tree.

And there's things
in piles

They're putting
things in piles,

pots and pans,
one still had
someone's supper
in it,

And clothes

Why?

She laughs.

Why the neat piles?

SHEANN: (*Softly, still struggling to breathe.*)
    What are
    the birds
    called?

CORDELIA: What?

SHEANN: The white
    birds.

    Trying to breathe.

    The bridge
    has gone,

    you can't
    get across,

    bits
    of it are
    sticking up
    from the
    river

    And the
    white birds
    are perched
    on the bits

    Are they
    seagulls?

    They aren't

    pigeons

    I was searching, –
    you know
    calling, –
    calling out
    my baby's name

and each time
the mad
white birds
flapped
and screamed

flying up in
the sky

So then I
stopped
calling

and it was
quiet then

and I saw
on the other
side of the
river

out of the
mud

in the
moonlight

a woman

I think
it was a
woman

she was
small and
faraway

a strange
old woman

like a
ghost,

watching me.

CORDELIA: (*Suddenly quiet and intense.*)
 You've got to forget
 about your daughter

 do you hear me?

 Stop looking for her.

 She's drowned

 As SHEANN rocks and moans and cries, calling her baby's name,
 CORDELIA starts to rub the sticks again.

CORDELIA: I had
 a daughter,
 if you
 must know.

 I went
 out on
 the piss
 with a client;

 came back
 drank a bottle of Krug,
 necked a dozen
 Williams' best oysters

 and we fucked.

 Didn't know
 I was pregnant
 till I gave birth
 on my own
 in the bathroom
 5 months later
 to this

 foetus,

 like a rat,
 skinned

in foul smelling
jelly.

I was
mortified

She stops rubbing the sticks.

I cut
the cord
with my
rose pruners,

tidied
myself up,

googling
all the time
of course
to find
the correct
way to do
things,
the best
way

I put...

I put
the dead thing,
in a shoe box,

made myself
a strong
black American

and went
into work.

A cloud slowly blots out the moonlight until they are in blackness.

Time passes... perhaps 6 months.

The mute chorus of women changes the acting areas... deft and almost invisible.

A meeting inside the put back together public building, but no lights now apart from a few small lanterns.

And the heat is oppressive.

HALL is standing, sweating, at the front. CORDELIA sits in the audience, fanning herself.

CORDELIA: We were promised
    government assistance...
    a rubble clearance
    and removal programme!

    Building materials, ...
    skilled and organised
    manpower…

    Portacabins...
    you know with
    gingham curtains
    at the window,

    whilst serious
    building work commenced
    on our homes

    Six months on, –
    the roads
    are still blocked
    with piles of broken furniture
    and cars.

    Who are we here?
    Now?

    She looks around.

Mm?
Sitting here?

Most of us
are professional people...
am I right?
Solicitors, dentists,
engineers, IT Specialists
teachers!

Yet we are still living...
forced to live,
like rats in shacks!

SOUND

Angry voices.

HALL: We don't have
the resources
at this moment.

CORDELIA: There's work happening
on other sites –

Sarcastically.

In other Zones

HALL: The Rebuild Programme
has been suspended...
adjusted ,throughout the UK
because of the continual
meteorological uncertainty

CORDELIA: So what you're saying
is that "The Powers That Be",
and by the way
we're not really sure
who they are anymore,

The shift shaping
Third Coalition

are not convinced
that our homes are
worth rebuilding

HALL: We have to make sure
that the limited resources
we have are channelled
into areas that are sustainable
and that rebuilding work is likely to endure

CORDELIA: *(Suddenly standing. Almost shouting.)*

Get used to living
on an urban dung heap
Ladies and Gentlemen!

Subsisting on fortnightly airdrops
of broken biscuits and biltong,

fighting over the one street tap

Law abiding, tax paying
citizens like you and I
who have spent a lifetime
serving, no enriching, our communities…

<u>our</u> homes
<u>our</u> humble amenities
<u>our</u> Lives...

Are not worth
rebuilding apparently!

SOUND

Uproar.

HALL: *(Raising his voice but calm, authoritative.)*
Calm down
calm down please and remain seated

SCENE 6

The river towpath. Moonlight.

CORDELIA is walking home after the meeting.

She stops, looks behind her as if she is being followed.

From ahead a menacing voice from the shadows...

VOICE: Your bag

> *CORDELIA seems to jerk her bag.*

Chuck it over

And no funny business

> *HALL steps out of the shadows, he looks sheepish.*

HALL: It's alright,
  It's alright
  Miss Standish
  It's only me...

  I needed
  to make
  a point.

> *Pause.*

CORDELIA: *(Coolly.)*

  A point
  Inspector?

HALL: If you're
  a woman
  and alone

  It isn't
  safe to walk
  along the
  towpath
  at night

it's better
that you have
a little scare
now than...
well

CORDELIA: I see

Thank you Inspector
for the lesson

HALL: You're cross

CORDELIA: No... no

though actually
you needn't
have worried

She "cocks" her straw bag.

You see
from the second
I saw you,
which was
a second
before you spoke

I had
my "Bulldog"
trained
on your bollocks

She takes out a small, very old gun from her bag.

and I am
a pretty good
shot.

You were
lucky,
very lucky.

The moon
came out

I saw
your face

otherwise
you might be...

She shrugs her shoulders.

Pause.

HALL: *(He laughs nervously.)*
Right...

He walks away... turns back.

Right.

Where did
you get it?

CORDELIA: It was
my father's...

HALL: Your father's?

CORDELIA: He was a
Major in

The 9th Royal
Lancers

and probably
my grandfather's.

It's
an heirloom.

HALL: And
is it
loaded?

CORDELIA: Of course.

HALL: How
did it survive
the floods?

CORDELIA: A completely
watertight
World War 2
box.

HALL: Impressive
but I'm afraid
you must
surrender it

Miss Standish

Pause.

CORDELIA: Rather
poor logic
Inspector

You
go to some
trouble to
expose my
assumed
vulnerability,

but

when it's apparent
I've taken sensible
steps to protect myself

you
disarm me.

HALL: *(Rueful.)*
Nevertheless…

CORDELIA: *(Quickly.)*
I'll drop

it off
somewhere
tomorrow

I'll say
I found
it in
the rubble

She smiles flirtatiously. Charmingly.

Wouldn't want
to make
a bulge
in your trousers

Inspector.

SOUND

A sudden flicker of light music. A party.

HALL: *(Frowning.)*
Is that
your
summer house?

CORDELIA: It's the
four walls
of my
summer house,

we don't
know where
the roof is.

HALL: *(Grimly.)*
Your young
lodger's
entertaining
then?

CORDELIA: What's
wrong with
that?

She found
some
friends who
survived the
storm,

they
play music
and dance.

She's 18
You forget
what it's
like to
be young
Inspector.

HALL: John
please
call me
John

CORDELIA: John?

Pause.

John Hall?

HALL: Not Ahmed
Patel or
Mamoud Singh,
you're thinking?

CORDELIA: Yes

HALL: John Hall
is my chosen
name

CORDELIA: I see

HALL: And...
   I was born
   in the United
   Kingdom

CORDELIA: I know,

   Finchley...

   And
   Born Again

   You see
   even in the
   last moments
   of Near Armageddon,
   people gossip.

She puts the gun away. She takes out a hip flask and after offering it to John she swigs from it.

On the
last still night

as the storm
clouds started
to silently form
to advance

surprising
everyone
with their
stealth

you
scaled
a cold
high mountain,

with nothing
but a litre

of vodka
and a
nice clean
hanky,

She laughs.

It
was
uncharitably
suggested
Inspector,
as I'm
sure you
are aware

you had
made for
the one place
in the
United Kingdom
the waves
couldn't conquer

Others believed
you meant
never to
come

down anyway

but you
did,

that next
morning,
to a
new world
reshaped
by the wind
and waves.

and you
had found

God

that's what
people say

Pause. She smiles.

A snowy God.

A tut... tutting
thin lipped
cold,
blue eyed
God,

who wagged
his icy
finger at
you

and told
you give
up
your stuff,

not that
you had

anything left...

just a
few pieces
of your
beloved

She pronounces, carefully.

chinoiserie

HALL: You mock
me

CORDELIA: Tease,
    I'm teasing
    you

    Slight pause.

    Are you
    married John?

HALL: I was, –
    at 18
    actually

CORDELIA: Do you
    have children?

HALL: My wife
    miscarried
    many times
    sadly,

    and then
    she left
    me so...

    no.

CORDELIA: And since...?

HALL: No-one
    really.

CORDELIA: No-one
    in all
    those years?

HALL: No-one
    significant

CORDELIA: You'll be
    telling me
    next that
    you're married
    to the force

HALL says nothing

CORDELIA: Well you've
    done very
    well John
    haven't you,
    really

    Very well
    Indeed

    Bravo!

HALL: *(Unsmiling.)*
    Yes
    Bravo indeed.

    Pause.

    And you?
    Are you...

CORDELIA: Married?
    Good God
    No.

    Flirtatious.

    Feel free
    to scrutinise
    my ring finger

    She holds it up and wiggles it.

HALL: As opposed
    to your
    trigger finger...

    Pause. They smile at each other.

CORDELIA: No,
    I am
    alone

in the world
John,

and
penniless,

my only asset
was my house ,

HALL: *He speaks softly.*
There's a
strict
no movement
policy between
Zones at the
moment

CORDELIA laughs.

But
I could
pull strings

get you placed
somewhere
marginally
more comfortable

perhaps
I could
help you
get a job...

an organisational
post...

CORDELIA: What...
shuffling paper
in a police
department?

I don't think so
do you?

HALL: Utilising
 your special skills,

 working
 with people...

 communicating.

 Our
 encounter
 this evening
 was...
 bruising

 You are a
 confident
 public speaker

 I admire that.

CORDELIA: No
 I'm staying
 here.

HALL: Why?

CORDELIA: It's my
 home,

 I own
 It

 I own
 the land

 I'm going
 to rebuild
 it.

HALL: Well
 Miss Standish...

CORDELIA: Cordelia

HALL: Yes

Cordelia *(Intensely.)*
You must
always
remember
that I
am your
friend.

She turns and looks out.

CORDELIA: It's
still beautiful.

HALL: Yes

CORDELIA: That's
why I'm
here,

the river.

Slight pause.

What
do you think
of the women?

HALL: What women?

CORDELIA: *(Surprised.)*
There's
a small
colony
now

on the
other side

busy...

HALL: Busy?

CORDELIA: Yes
living together

in what
used to be
the old
park
over there.

It's strange
I know
but sometimes
I think
they follow
me

HALL: *(Puzzled.)*
Women?

He looks over, carefully and sternly.

There
are no women
living on the
other side
of the
river.

FILM

Flickers into extreme close-up, thick undergrowth, we are looking down onto several pairs of solid shoes. We may be in some sort of bender. We might just catch sight of flames, a pot boiling... Steam or smoke.

The camera swings... We can just see a storm-rescued bit of buggy or pram. The blanket moves, we can't see what's inside. A pair of feet move towards it... We see a hand stirring a small bowl of something.

SCENE 7

SHEANN is sat in the almost dark. She is smoking, swigging lager from a tin. She is watching the film Soylent Green on an old TV with a cracked screen. She is eating crisps, when CORDELIA quietly enters – she tries to hide them.

CORDELIA: Right...
Well.
Hallo there

She stands in front of the screen, looking about suspiciously.

SHEANN: Hallo.

Pretending to be engrossed.

Could you...?

She gestures at CORDELIA to move out of the way of the screen.

CORDELIA: Is
it me,

or

is there
a funny
burny smell
in here?

Pause, SHEANN sniffs.

SHEANN: It's you.

No sorry
It's the
drains.

CORDELIA: It's
definitely
not the
drains

If
I
didn't know

it was
unlikely…

She inches closer to SHEANN.

I'd say, –
and this
is far-fetched
I agree

I'd say...

CORDELIA lunges at SHEANN, who yelps. She shoves her, revealing the treats.

Cigarettes!

Beer!

You've got
a tin of
lager

and you
never as
much offered
me
a swig

AND CRISPS!

You selfish
little cow!

Where you
get them?

SHEANN: None
of your
beeswax

Keep your
stuck up
nose

        out of
        my business

CORDELIA: I beg
        your pardon!

SHEANN: And
        don't call
        me selfish,

        that's rich
        coming from
        you

CORDELIA: I'm sorry?

SHEANN: How many
        tins of
        steak pudding

        have you
        had this
        week?

        Corned beef?

        Cocktail sausage
        and baked beans?

        A tin of
        jellied chicken!

        What you
        give me?

        What do
        I get?

        Day in
        day out –

        butter beans
        soya beans
        cut green beans

CORDELIA: A very
    good source
    of protein.

SHEANN: They make
    me fart

CORDELIA: Don't be
    vulgar please,

SHEANN: Spaghetti
    Alphabets...

CORDELIA: If you
    did some
    work around
    the place
    perhaps...

    you know
    got up
    off your
    skinny arse

SHEANN: Ooh!!
    Pot,
    Kettle
    black!

CORDELIA: I would
    consider
    improving
    your rations.

SHEANN: Oh...,
    would you
    Miss

    Really Miss?

    Thank you
    Thank you

Oh Great
White Lady!

CORDELIA: *(Flustered.)*
Look,
I have extended
generous hospitality
to you
my girl

SHEANN: Generous hospitality
my left tit!

CORDELIA: On the
implicit understanding
that you
would contribute

in some
way to
work on
house,

to rebuilding
the house.

SHEANN: You extended
generous hospitality
to me
Miss Cordelia Standish
in the
hope

that you'd
be getting

an unpaid
darkie

to do
all your

fucking old lady
dirty work.

"Sheann
the slop bucket
needs emptying"

"Sheann
the fire's dying
we need
more wood"

"Sheann
Go into town
and get the
water bottle
refilled..."

Sheann!
Sheann!
Sheann!

She screams.

I am
not your
maid

do you
understand?

I am
not your

laundry
hand

your water
fetcher

your porch
sweeper

I am
not your
slave!

Slight pause.

And I
am not
some poor
rescued
little girlie

who gets
paid peanuts,

to keep
a broke
burnt out
lonely
middle aged
bitch...
with no
friends, family
or man

company.

Hear me?

CORDELIA: *(Taking a deep breath. A tight smile.)*
The house
won't mend
itself Sheann,

jobs have
to get done

floorboards
have to be
nailed down
or they'll rot

we've got
cement now
to fill in
holes

I've gathered
all the
old tiles,

it's taken
me weeks,

we can
start putting
them on
the roof...

SHEANN: I can't
do all
that stuff

that
building-
climbing-
carrying-
shit

D'you hear
me?

You should
have got
yourself
a darkie
with a
dick!

Slight pause.

CORDELIA: Do you know
any?

Do you
know a
good one?

I mean
not a
darkie

any colour?

The colour's
irrelevant,
the dick
probably is
quite crucial
actually...

I'm an
experienced
project manager,

I've spent
my life in

property

I can't
pay them

but I
could offer
them a share
in the
rebuild.

SHEANN: We've got
a bog
haven't we?

electricity
couple of

hours a day

a telly!

an oven
that works
sort of

CORDELIA: Yes.

SHEANN: What's the
problem?

CORDELIA: And you're
happy are
you

Mm?

Quite happy
to live
like this
like this
for the
rest of
your life.

To live
like a
a...

SHEANN: What...?

Go on
say it
I dare
you.

A tits
out
lady nigger

squatting
in a
grass skirt

on the
telly

being spoke
nicely to

by some

fat
speccy

BBC dude.

No
I'm not
happy

if you
must know,

but it's
fun

watching
you up
to your
fucking
earrings
in shit!

CORDELIA: Look
we have
spades now.

SHEANN: Oh
Yippee!
Yippee!

CORDELIA: If we
dig
in the
slurry
who knows

what we
might find.

I mean
I had
nice stuff,

there's quality
stuff under
here –

a little
carriage clock
with a
diamond
crust,

A Hockney
print

dozens of vintage
Jimmy Choos

an
Aga!

A Xanski
fitted kitchen
with ice white
marble worktops
and ebony
finishings

A home cinema
complex with
seats from
Concorde

A basement pool
with a
rainforest party
room

There's a
silver Aston
Martin somewhere
out there…

For fuck's sake
I had
a gold
double strap
Rolex watch
worth...

SHEANN: If you
need money
Miss Standish

all you
have to
do is ask.

Not that
it has
any real
use anymore,

there being
like no
shops

SHEANN takes a roll of notes from her knickers.

SHEANN: There you
are

I think
you'll find
that'll pay
for my
Board and
Lodging

but I'm
not happy
with the
quality of
the breakfast

do you
hear me?

So no
more
frigging
butter beans.

SOUND

A police siren. A vehicle stops. footsteps.

They exchange looks.

The mute and invisible women change the setting.

SCENE 8

Police Station. Night. A side room.

SOUND

Mayhem.

CORDELIA is sitting. She is anxious. HALL enters.

HALL: You are
to be
charged with
brothel-keeping.

CORDELIA is speechless.

Your little friend,
and her friends
have been
"entertaining"

gentlemen in
the summer house

at the
bottom of
your garden

for some
months apparently.

CORDELIA: *(Laughs.)*
The minx.

Pause.

HALL: *(Mischievous.)*
They're happy
to move you
into the
old Red
Light District

CORDELIA: Don't tell
me

It's the
new
No Knickers
Zone.

HALL: *Smiling.*
Anyway
that is
not going
to be
necessary.

CORDELIA: Did you
know anything
about this?

HALL: Nothing

CORDELIA: Do they
　　know who
　　I am?

HALL: No...
　　no they
　　don't

　　Slight pause.

　　but I have
　　intervened
　　on your behalf

　　I told
　　you I
　　would be
　　a friend
　　to you,

CORDELIA: *(Relieved.)*
　　Thank you

　　No really
　　thank you

　　I
　　appreciate
　　that you
　　are an
　　important,
　　a very
　　important
　　and busy man
　　John,

　　especially in
　　these times

　　It's kind
　　of you
　　to offer

me your
assistance and
protection

I am
indebted
to you

HALL: He smiles.

You are
welcome

CORDELIA: *(An afterthought.)*
What will
happen to
Sheann?

HALL: I don't
think Prison
will be
a useful deterrent.

CORDELIA: Prison?
Really; Prison?
I thought
a fine
surely

a Caution?

HALL: She will
be tried
in the
new courts,
and if
found guilty,

I will
recommend
she serves
her sentence

in one
of our
New Time
Out Zones.

FILM

*Film flickers into – Several pairs of feet... then camera swings – to
a long shot of a completely empty street – on both sides are imposing
government buildings.*

SCENE 9

Night. CORDELIA's house.

*CORDELIA is seated. On her knees, the shoe box. She takes off the lid.
She has trouble breathing.*

Inside a tiny skeleton.

FILM

Close up of a female hand carefully unlocking a door.

SCENE 10

Night. The Ruins of a Church. Shadow of a grille – a confessional.

HALL: *(He whispers.)*
   I didn't want
   to be
   a good man

   I wanted
   to be
   a successful one.

   I wanted
   to be a
   powerful man

   I wanted to be
   admired

envied...
desired

feared!

That most
especially,

that
brought me
the most
satisfaction.

And to
become
this most
feared and
successful man,

I aspired
to the
top job,
the
fastest car,

the biggest
house,
stuffed full
of
things

I consumed
from breath
to breath,
leaving a
trail of
waste and
bad words
and tears.

I valued
my body

because it
brought me
pleasure,

my mind,
because
it allowed
me to
outwit and
outmanoeuvre

my spirit
was bursting...
straining to
expand to
fit all
the excess,

and
my soul –
without space
started to
shrivel
like a nut
in sand.

I was
truly
a fallen man,

lying
on a cold
mountain side
under the
screaming storms
and winds
waiting
for the end.

But...
a miracle happened

I was
given
an opportunity

to start
again

to start
again.

And I
will try

I will try

to do
things better.

I will try

God
sent the raging
wind and waves
to cleanse
and purify

and
He will send

the scorching sun.

SCENE 11

Time has passed in moving shadows. Perhaps 3 years.

Time Out / Exclusion Zone. A light airy room. Bright sunshine through a window.

CORDELIA waits. Her appearance is altered. No make up or done hair. She wears very simple slightly grubby slacks, boots, a worn looking top and jacket.

SHEANN enters. She is dressed in clean simple clothes.

But

She is dreadfully changed.

The skin on her face and hands looks burnt and disfigured, her lips swollen, one eye is bloodshot and appears half closed.

Her gait too is strange, as if she is in pain.

SHEANN: You
    look rough.

    CORDELIA, horrified and astonished, can't find words.

CORDELIA: I...

SHEANN: I thought
    you'd forgotten
    about me

CORDELIA: No...
    No...
    I've been
    busy

SHEANN: For 3 years?

    CORDELIA is trying to process what she sees.

What's
been happening

Have you
built the
house back?

CORDELIA: A room,

I've got
a room
now.

SHEANN: With
a door?

CORDELIA: Yes,
it locks
as well

SHEANN: That's good

CORDELIA: Yes...
I, er
used the
money you
er...
gave me

SHEANN: Yeah
right!

I should
have got
that back.

CORDELIA: Well
I'm treating
it as a
loan

you know
15% interest

SHEANN laughs.

Anyway,
I found
a one armed
builder

and

labour's
cheap now

but then...

SHEANN: The money
ran out.

Pause.

Did you
miss me?

CORDELIA: Hardly

SHEANN: *(Laughing.)*
You did,
you really
did.

SHEANN leans in. She smiles, puts her hand on her lips, then takes out a small whistle from her dress, and blows into it, gently at first, then loudly.

She gestures that CORDELIA should join her kneeling down in a corner of the room.

CORDELIA: What the...?

SHEANN: *(Whispering.)*

It's bugged
in here

supposed
to be

but it
dun't pick
up the
corners.

They hear
the whistle
and think
it's a
malfunction

She laughs.

Clever eh?

I've something
for you

From under her dress she takes out a small plastic box. She gives it to CORDELIA.

Open it

CORDELIA opens it.

CORDELIA: Oh my…

SHEANN: Ssh!

CORDELIA: Bacon

A bacon
sandwich

SHEANN: Sorry
it's cold

and a
slice of
apple pie,
see

homemade

CORDELIA: I'm starving.

They've cut
rations
right down

SHEANN: Eat.
They're yours

A ravenous CORDELIA tucks in.

CORDELIA: *(Mouth full.)*

Don't you
want any?

SHEANN: No

CORDELIA: I...
I felt
guilty you
know about
when you
were my
guest

SHEANN: Your guest?

Oh yeah

CORDELIA: I thought
if I
had tried
to feed
you better,

If I
had been
a more
generous host,

you wouldn't...

you know

have...

SHEANN: Oh I would,
   I would have

   I've always
   done it see

   like since
   I was 13

   since Lillian
   died.

CORDELIA: Lillian?

SHEANN: My foster mum
   She was really
   nice.

   Used to hit
   me with a
   belt and
   sing me to
   sleep.

   Slight pause.

   Anyway
   they put
   me back
   in care
   see

   but

   I ran away

   ended up
   on the
   streets,

   met Mr Jefferson
   who mended Lillian's
   washing machine
   once

and I went
to live
with him

and then
he sold
me to
Richard
who ran
quite a few
girls
down here.

CORDELIA has stopped eating.

CORDELIA: *(Astonished.)*
Sold you...

He sold you?

SHEANN: Yes

CORDELIA: But
no! no!
how can
that be
no!

SHEANN: I was only
13

CORDELIA: A child

SHEANN: Oh there
was younger
than me

and
Richard

was actually
quite a

decent
bloke

CORDELIA: Right.

She is horrified and distressed.

SHEANN: Don't you
    want the
    pie?

CORDELIA: You have
    it

SHEANN: I don't
    want it

    I get
    a hot
    meal at
    6

    Lasagne...?

    Toad in
    the hole...?

    Fish 'n Chips...?

    Then after
    they let
    us

    watch a film
    on telly

    This used
    to be
    the old
    Social Security
    building

    It's huge
    there's loads

of nice
rooms left...

with sofas
and wallpaper

They've made
a little
garden for
us out
of the
ruined bit

We can
walk around
chat

Most of the
girls are
a right laugh

We share
rooms, I
share with
a girl called
Porcupine...

There's air
conditioning!
and they
let you
personalise it,

and get this –

every night

the guards
come in
and give
you a

milky drink!

And
they'll give
you a
packet of
fags for
a fuck.

Let you
smoke it
on the
fire escape.

It's not
too bad
in here
actually.

CORDELIA: What...
What happened
to your...

Skin..?

Your

face?

SHEANN: Oh I
agreed to
sign up
to a
programme

They put
me in a
room and
I have
to sit in
front of a

very bright
white light

and when
I can't
take it
no more

I press
a buzzer

and they
turn it
off.

CORDELIA listens.

There's lots
of different
stuff you
can do.

One girl
climbs into
a tank
of
water...

I think

or something

I don't
want to
do that.

CORDELIA: No
of course
not

SHEANN: And they
pay you, –

like a
proper salary,

you
get it every
week in a
little pink
envelope

Pause.

CORDELIA: Right.

SHEANN: *(Quieter still.)*
I don't
touch them

I keep
them for
Sascha

For my baby

They've
promised to
look through
records for
me.

They've promised
to look
for her

I know
what you
think

but some
babies
were found
alive

and they've
got them
somewhere

CORDELIA: What do
you mean?

SHEANN: They've
kept them

CORDELIA: Where...?
Somewhere
like this?

SHEANN: I dream
about her

every night.

Sometimes
she's grown
a
fish tail

and she
chats about
her life
under the
water with
the other
fishes

Sometimes
she's still
a tiny baby

waving happily
at me
from the
waves.

They're going
to

help
me
find her

They are

They promised

CORDELIA: Right

SHEANN: *(Leaning even closer.)*
Remember
those women?

CORDELIA: What women?

SHEANN: From the
other side
of the
river

CORDELIA: Yes
of course
Yes

SHEANN: I think
they come
here

you know

in here

in secret.

Sometimes
they drug
the guards, ...

come in
at night

CORDELIA: Why?

SHEANN: *(Shrugs her shoulders.)*

They film
what's going
on...

SCENE 12

Time passes. No more than a few days.

HALL's office. By his uniform, we can tell he has been promoted. And he is smarter, sharper.

HALL: *(Cold, angry.)*

Well
I don't believe
her!

It is
extremely difficult
to obtain
the post
of a Guard
in the
Time Out
Zones.

They are
scrupulously
vetted

Do you
really think
a man,
a family man
probably,
is going
to risk
his precious
job
for 5 minutes
on a fire escape

with a...
a...

CORDELIA: A what
John...?

Pause.

But you
will look
into it?

HALL: Of course
I will

And if
there has
been
sexual
impropriety

Cordelia laughs.

at any level
they will be
removed,

I promise
you that.

Pause.

CORDELIA: Thank you

Pause.

And what
about...
The Programme?

HALL: What about it?

CORDELIA: Her place
on the
programme.

HALL: *(Pause.)*
>The Scientific
>Community,

>are desperate
>to understand
>the implications
>of the predicted
>climate variations
>for ordinary
>people.

>Computer
>studies before
>The Storms

>proved unreliable

>And now
>The risk assessors
>The statisticians
>The number crunchers
>call them
>what you
>like

>arrive at different
>conclusions depending
>on who you speak
>to and when.

>It is so frustrating.

>But what is clear ,
>is that
>every sector
>of society
>will be affected,

>and we
>have to be

armed with
as much
information
we can reasonably
gather, to
ensure the
best chance
of survival
for the
Citizens of
The United
Kingdom.

To protect
the future,
the future
of our
children

and it
is proving
impossible
to do this
efficiently

with microbes
in a petri dish

or
rats
in a laboratory

CORDELIA: You mean
they keep
dying.

HALL: Of course
it isn't
ideal,

no one's
pretending
that,

I take
my part
in this
operation

seriously

very seriously
indeed

I have
a moral
responsibility
to support
The Government
in their
decisions

And the programme
provides a

protected
and easily monitored
study group who
are willing to
embrace a

small risk...

CORDELIA: Oh so you
accept there's
a risk...

HALL: ...for the
good of society...
at large...

Slight pause.

Look,
the risks
are minimised

no
one is forced
onto the programme

against their will

they volunteer

CORDELIA: What are
their options,

living half
starved
in a filthy shack
year in year out?

Slight pause

Are men
prisoners
invited onto
the programme?

HALL: Yes of course,
there is no
sexual discrimination

CORDELIA: *(Laughing.)*
What are
the long
term effects
on the
woman's health
with these
experiments?

Does anyone know?

Sarcastic.

Has anyone
conducted
a risk assessment?

HALL: We expect
them to make
a full
recovery

CORDELIA: What are
the other
experiments?

HALL: Sorry?

CORDELIA: Sheann says
there are
Time Out Zones

exclusively for
pregnant women,

That there
is a lot
of secrecy...

CORDELIA starts to semi-collapse.

I mean
are there
Time Out Zones
exclusively
for disabled
people?

are there?

or gay
people?

What about
babies John?

What are
you doing
to them?

Pause.

HALL: *(Coldly.)*
You are
hysterical
Cordelia

I am

disappointed
in you

Pause.

Can I
get you
some water?

CORDELIA: Yes. Thank you.

HALL carefully pours a tumbler of water from a glass jug, hands it to CORDELIA.

HALL: It's ridiculous
a woman
of your background

choosing

to live
such a
life.

Look
at you

What's
happened to
your hands?

Pause.

CORDELIA: *(Softly.)*
   I cannot
   even start
   to rebuild
   my house
   entirely
   on my
   own

   I have tried
   and I can't

   She takes his hand.

   I need
   materials of course,

   but most
   of all

   I need
   labour,

   not much
   and not
   for long,

   3 or 4
   men

   for a month
   maybe 2

   Pause.

   I need help
   I need your help

   She kisses him, tenderly, sweetly, sexually.

   Long pause.

   He does not return her kiss.

Am I
no longer
attractive
to you
John?

He does not reply.

We know
there is
something
between us

something
sweet and strong

My father
was a modest man

You have
gentle eyes

Softer still.

And I
love your
burnished skin
I...

She starts to slide her hands into his trousers.

Gently, sensitively he extricates himself.

HALL: *(Pause.)*
  I am
  on the
  short list

  for a
  new appointment

  a promotion

If I
am successful

I will
be moving
shortly,

attached to
National Security
in The Central Zone.

It is
very important
when my
records are
minutely examined,

which they will be,

I am found
to be

above reproach
on every issue.

I hope
you
understand

I can
hardly
condemn
corruption
in my officers

and then
found
to be

entangled

doling out
favours to
a... a...

CORDELIA: Friend.

Pause.

No
of course not

HALL: I <u>can</u> tell you
because
It's no great
secret,
that Zone 6
your Zone

will become
a Work Zone,

part of
The Rebuild
Programme

Thousands
of construction
workers in
cabins will
be moved in

to rebuild
the bridges
and the banks,

It won't
be legal
to live there

CORDELIA: *(A tense pause.)*
We will
see about that

HALL: *(He sighs, suddenly impatient.)*
    You will be
    accountable
    to the law
    Cordelia,

CORDELIA: What
    about the
    promises
    you made
    to her?

HALL: Promises?

CORDELIA: To look
    through records
    to see
    if her
    daughter is
    still alive.

    Don't you
    remember?

    She's desperate
    to find
    her daughter

    I think
    she's been
    driven
    half mad

HALL: We will
    keep them,
    of course.

SCENE 13

Time passes in moving shadows. Perhaps six months.

CORDELIA's house.

She is looking out over the river. She is in some distress. She has the gun in her hand. But she has trouble gripping because of the damage to her hands. She tries a practice shot into the air, but she can't get enough force through her fingers. She tries again and again becoming more frustrated.

FILM

Projected over the image of CORDELIA with the gun –

Long shot... a large group of women standing on the River's Edge.

CORDELIA sweating stands with the gun in her trembling hand. She points it into her mouth. But she does not have the force in her finger to pull the trigger. She tries again. And again.

SCENE 14

Time passes in moving shadows. Perhaps six months.

Darkness. Candlelight. SHEANN is seated, her face cannot be seen. CORDELIA, also in darkness and in silhouette, is changing.

CORDELIA: There are
    600 portacabins,

    not too
    close together.

    There are no
    bars or cafes,

    no clubs

    no common
    meeting areas
    at all

    So,

the only possible
strategy is to
knock on the
door.

SHEANN: *(Laughing.)*

You're off your head

CORDELIA: We know
they are all
single young
men

We know
they are
all construction
workers

It's what
used to
be called

Targeted
Sales.

SHEANN: We both
go in

CORDELIA: The cabins
have a
curtained
sleeping area

SHEANN: Always get
the money
first

CORDELIA: No, I've
told you
materials
will do

or labour

SHEANN: On a
    promise?

CORDELIA: Deferred payment

SCENE 15

In front of the women, HALL stands. He is in a tuxedo, sweating profusely.
He is speaking to The Federation, using some notes.

HALL: And
    of course
    any job
    presents challenges

    But equally
    let's not
    be shy
    of our
    successes...

    which er
    incidentally
    doesn't
    include our
    air conditioning
    in here
    this evening

    Low voice.

    Can somebody
    look into
    that please?

    He swallows, he has lost his place in the notes.

    During the last year

we have
experienced
no fewer

than 5
no 6
Major Red
Alert incidents

And
while these
resulted in
one tragic
loss of life

of a much
revered
public figure,

they were
humanely
and
effectively
suppressed
without
major casualties.

The light on him is starting to flicker.

Perhaps...

Perhaps
my most recent
notable achievement

in this
office

has been
has been...

Pause.

not the
er
Return to
Full Power
Initiative
obviously

He laughs.

aspiring to
a level
of... of...

His notes are in the wrong order.

transparency

and...

public accountability

in all
areas;

Never forgetting

that we...
we...

Slight pause.

And
We seem
to have
gremlins in
our electrics
this evening...

Gentlemen.

He swallows. He can't find the right place in his notes.

He stops.

His speech has ended with a thundering silence.

HALL looks embarrassed.

SCENE 16

Time passes in moving shadows. Perhaps a year.

CORDELIA in moonlight and SHEANN in the shadows, stand in front of The House. Occasionally they swig from a bottle of wine, which they share.CORDELIA looks looser, taken apart, SHEANN in a business like suit and scarf, tighter and put together .

CORDELIA: We will instruct
    the architect
    to respect the
    footprint of
    the old house

    but build up
    and out
    skeletal
    over the river.

    He'll work
    with glass
    and found objects.

    He has a yard
    somewhere,

    with Persian
    tiles,

    Victorian stained
    glass

    and
    Jacobean beams.

SHEANN: How can
    we afford
    him?

CORDELIA: If he's
    hungry
    we'll feed him

    Ill flatter him

    I'll fuck him.

    Silence.

SHEANN: One day
    Lillian took
    me to
    the park

    There was
    a sandpit
    and a
    boating lake,

    She'd made
    me a
    sunsuit

    That's what
    she called
    it
    out of
    some bint's
    skirt she
    cared for.

    It had
    daft yellow
    ducklings
    on it
    in spotted
    red bow ties.

    She bought
    me a

space rocket
ice lolly

and plaited
buttercups in
my hair

It was
the happiest
day of my
life

When I
was being
fucked and
it was
gross and
it hurt,
and it made
me feel
sick

I always
used
to think
of that
day

CORDELIA: Are the
books up
to date?

SHEANN says nothing.

Every visit
needs to be
logged –
recorded –
invoiced

SHEANN: It's difficult
for me

CORDELIA: I can't
    do everything...

SHEANN: I don't mind
    answering the phone

    I don't mind
    opening the door

    I like
    taking the money

    I cant stand
    the
    what...?
    The
    book keeping -
    Its...

    I don't know
    It upsets me,

    Pause.

CORDELIA: Are they
    up
    to date?

SHEANN: Yes
    they are
    they really are.

CORDELIA: *(Relieved.)*
    Good

    Well done

    They both look out over the river.

    Shouting suddenly.

    Fuck off
    You dirty
    witches

SHEANN: *Softly.*
　What you
　doing?

　Shut up.

　Shut up!

CORDELIA: Well
　Its none
　of their business.

FILM

Film flickers... close up on the eyes of a child (about 4) with the women looking up and out.

SCENE 17

Time passes with moving shadows. Perhaps five years.

Hot evening. CORDELIA's house has been rebuilt in the style of an ultra-modern hacienda with a sweeping stairway, balconies and porches covered in pink frothing, flowering blossom everywhere, pots of flowers and shrubs, even a vine with plump, juicy, grapes.

It is early evening – a roasting summer. The heat of the day is just subsiding, the air is thick and warm.

A coat rail shows police uniform jackets hanging... boots and hats.

SOUND

In an upper room, a party, male and female voices... much laughter.

SHEANN enters. She is dressed elegantly, simply, expensively; her hair is neat and pretty.

But for the first time, we realise her face has been significantly disfigured during her time on the Time Out programme, permanently swollen and she is blind in one eye.

Standing in the shadows is HALL. SHEANN hears him. She looks about. She sees him.

HALL: Is it you?

Pause.

SHEANN: I don't know
I'll ask myself.

Softly.

And
why wouldn't
you recognise
me
Inspector?
Commander?

She smiles.

Inspector

HALL: It's...

It's been
many years

SHEANN: *(With humour, mischevious.)*
Oh yes
of course

Pause.

HALL is staring at her.

HALL: *(Upset, struggling.)*
I'm sorry
I'm so...

SHEANN: And
I'm not
the only one
who's changed

She looks at him from top to toe. He is out of uniform, casually dressed, he looks displaced

Pause.

You took
your new broom
into their dusty
little corners
we heard

HALL: Perhaps

SHEANN: So now
you're back

SOUND

Voices. Laughter.

SHEANN: She did
it.

She gestures.

She rebuilt
the house

Aren't you
interested
in how?

HALL: No...
No...
I'm not

SHEANN: Offends your
sensibilities
Inspector Hall?

The Programme
did me
a good turn
as it
happens

If I
was still
pretty

I'd be
up there

flat on
my back
now

with a
sweaty
lump
on top
of me

pumping
away.

Nobody
really wanting
me

has left
me free

to
project manage.

He turns away.

Softer.

She was
quite a hit, –

Well you
can imagine –

with the
construction
workers.

Eventually I
was able to
cut down
her visits,

developing the
summer house
first
was my idea

There was
no shortage
of enterprising
girls wanting
to invest
in a new
venture

Once that
was established

I called
in favours

old friends
of ours Inspector
yours and
mine

mutual Friends

HALL: *(Fierce, rattled.)*
Shut up.
I don't
want to
hear that

and
I am back

I am back
now

I will
close the
place down,
you do
realise that
don't you?

SHEANN: No you
won't,

you see
the same
blokes
who got you
kicked out
of National Security

are our
very best
clients

HALL: *(Agitated.)*
It's illegal

This is
a work zone

SHEANN: Not for
them it
i'nt

Ever heard
don't shit
in your own
backyard

They like
crossing the river

It's their
very own
Private Party Zone

Pause.

SOUND

Laughter. Voices.

SHEANN: And are
you here
for business
Inspector?

HALL: Don't be
ridiculous.

SHEANN: *(Mischievous.)*
Not Cordelia surely?
Surely?

HALL: Poor lady.
She doesn't
belong to
this world.

SHEANN: And I
do of course!

At least
she had
a choice,

bending over
and taking
it up
the arse

in't worse
at 40
than 13

SOUND

Laughter. Voices.

CORDELIA appears, older, looking strained and tired even fragile, but dressed to be alluring now and provocative.

HALL steps back into the shadows.

CORDELIA: *(To SHEANN.)*

> The sun's
> hot and
> you've no
> hat

She kisses her tenderly on the cheek.

SOUND

> *Laughter, music, voices.*

SHEANN: You look
> tired.

> *SHEANN strokes her face.*

> They've got
> Marie and
> Suzanne

> The big
> man always
> stinks

> Why doesn't
> someone
> tell him?

CORDELIA: Everyone's
> afraid

> That's what
> power must
> smell like

Pause.

SHEANN: You're shaking

CORDELIA: I'm melting

SHEANN: *(Strokes her hair, kisses her hand.)*

> Stan's found
> some lamb
> can you
> believe it?

CORDELIA: It's too
> hot to
> eat

SHEANN: Finish off

> You're not
> working tonight

CORDELIA: No?

SHEANN: No

> I won't
> let you

SHEANN leads CORDELIA off, she glances into the shadows.

SCENE 18

The river towpath. Moonlight.

Night.

CORDELIA stands looking out over the river. She has a brandy glass.

HALL appears from the shadows.

CORDELIA: *(She doesn't look at him.)*
> They've gone

> *Pause.*

HALL: Who?

CORDELIA: The women,
the women
over there

who watched
us...

followed us...
sometimes.

Overnight

they've disappeared

HALL: *(Puzzled, he talks softly.)*
Have they?

I'm not
aware of
any women
living over
there.

CORDELIA: They dug
tunnels we
think

when the
trees died

HALL: Tunnels?
No the
ground's too
soft...

CORDELIA: I shouted
at them

Cursed them

Perhaps they
despised me

Anyway

What does
it matter
now?

It's too
late now

Pause.

And you're
back
Sheann told me

HALL: Yes it's
been a
while.

CORDELIA: You were...
out of
your depth

we heard

Pause.

He moves in close to her, – an intimacy.

HALL: *(Softly.)*
You rebuilt
the house.

CORDELIA: On my back,

I fucked
for bricks,

and crap, –

twiddly gold
leaf frames,
for pastoral
scenes, –
cows in fields,

She laughs

a Georgian
four Poster –
nymphs
and a great
sea serpent
carved in
blackened oak

And a bowl, –
my pride and
joy,

venetian glass

It floated
in the floods
they told me

I let
a poor young lad
with bottle green eyes
and a rotting crotch

fist me for that.

Pause. She laughs

Sometimes

I wish the waves
would come again
and wash it all
away.

Pause.

How hot
will it get,

this year,
the next?

What's
happening
about the
drought?

People know
we've got
clean water
here

They come
at night
break into the kitchen
and steal it
in buckets

and pans

He takes her hand, puts her fingers to his mouth, tenderly.

What's
happening
to the river?

It's a
little brook

in some parts

He kisses her fingers.

covered in
moss and algae.

In some
light

you imagine
you could
walk across

He puts his arms around her, tries tenderly to hold her, to kiss her.

She breaks free, angry.

You never
helped her

HALL: What?

CORDELIA: Sheann.
She went
on the
programme
because
your men
promised
they'd find
her baby.

HALL: I'm sure
they tried

There were
thousands of
babies
lost in
the storms

CORDELIA: She's sterile

HALL: I'm sorry

CORDELIA: But
not surprised!

So are
all the
young women
from the
programme

She cries
out every
night in
her sleep

Every day
she goes
to the river
to search

on the
child's birthday
her breast's
produce milk

HALL: I want
to help you,
don't you see?

seeing you
so broken

I want
to offer you
my tender
protection

I'm an
odd man
some might
say a cold man

but tenderness

a need
to protect,
a woman

a beautiful
cultured clever
woman such
as yourself

this is a
new feeling

A wonderful feeling.

CORDELIA drinks the brandy, then goes to the river's edge, and fills the glass.

CORDELIA: Look, see
the river
water

It's full
of these

little shits.

See them

swimming
about like mad.

They're tiny

but they're
fierce

and they're
multiplying,

every evening
more and

more

She is holding the glass up to the moonlight.

We see the swarming Protozoa.

SCENE 19

Public meeting.

HALL: Well
of course
we are
investigating

Marine ecologists
are working round

the clock
but it is
proving very
challenging

as soon
as one
strategy appears
to be working

the organisms
develop resistance.

And yes
the smell
is offensive.

My advice...

My advice...
is at certain
times of the
day to stay
inside, away
from the
river,
well away if
you can,

if possible

Stay upwind

SOUND

Hoots of aggressive and derisive laughter.

Wear masks ,
tie a scarf
round your mouth and throat.

CORDELIA and SHEANN arrive late, they try and sit discreetly.

An awkward and aggressive silence.

They are seated.

Then a female voice from the crowd says...

VOICE: Whores
    are not welcome
    at this meeting

   The mute and invisible women, now many, make changes.

SCENE 20

CORDELIA's garden. Moonlight.

CORDELIA and SHEANN stand in front of a freshly dug grave.

SHEANN takes the lead gun box. She takes out the gun.

CORDELIA puts the little mummified body of her dead baby, now wrapped in muslin, and places it in the box. She locks it.

Together they place the box into the grave. SHEANN fills in with earth.

CORDELIA: I was
    always afraid
    if I buried
    her

    the foxes
    might get
    her

SHEANN: Not
    in that box.

    She's safe
    now,

    poor little
    born bones

CORDELIA: *(She is silently crying.)*
    In all
    these years

I have not
shed a
single tear

for my
dead
daughter

With a finger, SHEANN lifts a single tear from CORDELIA's face.

CORDELIA: *(Takes out a cross.)*

I'll change
the wooden
cross for
a silver one
one day

SHEANN: Not now

It'll get
stolen

*SHEANN takes another small wooden cross identical to the one held
by CORDELIA.*

CORDELIA: What's that?

SHEANN: For Sascha

CORDELIA: But you
don't believe
she's dead

SHEANN: All these
years
I felt
her close
to me

Sometimes
when the
sun comes
up and

shines on
the water

I hear
her singing

Sometimes
in the moonlight
quite far
away on
the other
side of
the river
bank

I think
I see
her dancing
in the mist

But it's
all stopped

She's gone

I think
she's gone
forever

CORDELIA takes the cross and replaces it with a stone.

CORDELIA: We'll put
a stone
for each
lost year

And we'll
hope

The two women closely and lovingly embrace.

SHEANN: What about the gun?

FILM

Film flickers into a small brook, running water, a young brown hand is filling a small container. The camera swings up to the sky, fleetingly showing the back of her head and countryside. The hand makes a hole in the earth, fills it with water, pushes a small green shoot and then pats the earth around it.

SCENE 21

Candlelight.

HALL is slumped forward in a chair, his hands clasped in front of him – a very English semi-prayer position.

CORDELIA and SHEANN are crouched in front of the Venetian glass bowl. It is full of the river water, jelly like now.

At HALL's feet, a nearly empty bottle of vodka.

HALL: *(Very drunk.)*
  So you come
  down the
  mountain alright –

  secrets
  like stones
  everywhere –

  state secrets
  like thorns
  under bare feet

  meetings
  underground
  whispered behind
  grilles

  long dark
  winding brick tunnels

  Guards
  called Moles

He laughs.

with their
special
see your soul
blue light
technology

deeper
and
deeper

Down to
the sewers

117
character and digit
Security Access code

deeper
and
deeper

CORDELIA: *(Looking into the bowl.)*
There's millions
of them
but they've
nowhere to go
nowhere to swim
with the river dry

So they shit,
poison the
last bottom
bit of the water

And then
they die

SHEANN: They're
eating
each other.

HALL: Suddenly beautiful –

A mosaic
on the
tunnel walls

The Story
of Man

So surprising
So touching

A caveman
sat round
the first fire
roasting ox
pleased with himself

The ruffed Elizabethan
declaiming from
his scroll

A bearded gent
in a suit
peering
into a
microscope

Suddenly

the path widens
and the floor
is concrete now

and the blue
and yellow tiles

show London
on fire,
flames
behind St Paul's

you realise

the secret vastness
of it all.

SCENE 22

Time passes in moving shadows. Perhaps two years.

Unbelievable white hot sunshine.

CORDELIA's house.

All the plants and even the vine are dead.

A figure is lying down covered in blankets. It is apparent that whoever is under the blankets is gravely ill.

SHEANN returns.

SHEANN: What?

You're boiling...

She pulls all the blankets off. It is CORDELIA. She is semi-conscious, unable to speak.

SHEANN: *(Whispers urgently.)*
Wake up!
Wake up now!

She takes a small bottle of water. She drips it into CORDELIA's mouth.

A glass is empty by CORDELIA's side. She fills it with the water then takes a sachet out of her bag, mixes it carefully in the water.

If you
knew how
much this
cost you'd
wake up

She tries to get her to drink from the glass very slowly, a sip at a time.

There's no
drugs left

no proper
ones

You should
see the crowds
outside the
hospital

There's lines
of police
in helmets
with shields
and batons

I thought
she won't
like that

She wipes her face.

Everyone's ill,
and there's
loads dead

most of
the construction
workers –
our poor
young men

and its
all because
of the river –

the stinking
water.

Soldiers
are carrying
them out
of the
cabins

putting them
on the back
of lorries

tossing them
into graves

on the edge
of town.

Softer still and more scared. She wets a cloth and dabs CORDELIA's face.

And
you can
hardly walk
on the towpath

It's full of
the swollen
dead river
creatures

I mean
trillions and
trillions

FILM

Film flickers... a young brown hand is packing a rucksack... The camera swings up for a second, we see other women in long grass packing, ready to leave...

SCENE 23

HALL's office.

He is alone, sweating, red-faced, his shirt undone. Perhaps he too is ill.

He talks into his police radio, which spits and crackles. We hear a vast angry protesting crowd

HALL: (*Softly, calmly.*)
  Yes

if they have
ignored all
warnings
Yes

He waits. He is still.

SOUND

Very far away gun shots. Screams and cries.

SHEANN moves from the shadows.

HALL: *(Astonished.)*
How is it
possible?

How could
you get
in here?

SHEANN: I am
invisible
John,

He makes to press an alarm button.

Cordelia is
ill

She's dying.

He stops and listens.

I can't
get the
drugs

And
we've no
clean water

just a
couple of
bottles

Food's running
out

HALL: Like every
citizen then

SHEANN: Not quite

She takes out a wad of notes.

HALL laughs.

And you
have feelings
for her,

for Cordelia,

unbelievably

you have
true and tender
feelings for her

SOUND

We hear shots and cries then screams.

For a moment, SHEANN and HALL both stand and listen horrified.

Then HALL sinks into a chair.

HALL: *(Slight pause.)*
Did you
tell her
about me?

Ever?

Pause.

SHEANN: What?

HALL: About me!

SHEANN: That you
were a
client?

A friend
of Richard's?

A regular?

One of
my first
regulars

for a few
years, –
till I got
too old
of course,
for your
very
particular
tastes

HALL: I thought
she might
save me.

I thought
as I was
a Fallen
Man and
she a Fallen
Woman,
a real grown
woman

we
might save
each other

SHEANN: No

I never told
her.

It has
been our
secret

<u>SOUND</u>

The crowd is getting louder. More shots, screams, cries...

HALL: *(Softly.)*
When I
I went up

the mountain

on the
last still
night

it was
to save
myself

from the
storm
perhaps

But it was
to put
myself in
God's hands

<u>SOUND</u>

More shots, more screams.

And
a strange thing
happened, –

I woke up

SHEANN: I don't
    want to
    hear this

HALL: I filled my lungs
    with the pure
    thin air, the
    oxygen, and
    my brain
    suddenly cleared,

SHEANN: I don't
    want to
    hear all
    your fucking
    top of
    the mountain
    crap

HALL: And the
    light was
    new as if
    it was the
    first day
    of the world

    Of a
    new
    life

SHEANN: Shut up.

HALL: And I
    sensed
    something
    Bigger...

    Greater...

    I sensed
    that God

had forgiven
me

SHEANN: Well I
don't forgive you.

Do you hear me?

HALL: And I
came down
the mountain
with everything
changed

SHEANN: Nothing changed
nothing changed

HALL: And soon
after

God sent
the Storm
and the
world changed

SHEANN: Millions died
I lost
my baby
I lost
my baby

HALL: and it was
a new
beginning

SHEANN: It was
an end
a stupid
pointless end

HALL: A chance
to do things

better, this
time.

SHEANN: You missed
that chance

Pause.

HALL: I thought...
I thought
I had
got away
with it
you see,

SHEANN: You missed
that chance

Instead
you remade
the future
from a
rotting past

HALL: I thought
my terrible
shameful past
had been
drowned
and
blown away

Until...

SHEANN: Until...?

HALL: That
night you
walked
naked into
the meeting.

I should
have known
that you
were sent
by God

as a warning

as a reminder

<u>SOUND</u>

A huge surging crowd.

I was
removed
from National
Security because
I was shown
something that
I couldn't
reconcile with
my conscience
I tried
but I couldn't ,

I want
to show
it to
you

Will you
come with
me?

SHEANN: Will you
     give me the
     medicine...
     the water?

HALL: Yes
     I will

Pause.

SHEANN: *(Fearful.)*

> What is
> it?

FILM

Film flickers into close up of many feet... also small brown feet in sandals walking along what was the river bank. The feet stop. We see a puddle of stagnant water, a green gelatinous mess.

SCENE 24

At the highest point. HALL and SHEANN.

Blackness. A beam of white light illuminates them.

When they speak, their voices echo as in a vast underground cave.

SHEANN: *(Fierce. Astonished. Indignant.)*

> Is this it?
> Mm?
>
> Is this
> The Secret?
>
> It's just a
> warehouse
>
> It's just
>
> STUFF!

HALL: *(Softly, very quickly, agitated.)*

> This store
> supplies
> Zone 6,
>
> your Zone.
>
> In the front
> you see fuels
> barrels and barrels.

Petrol, diesel.

even coal

You see the
household generators?

The small solar
wind turbines.

Beyond them
the medical supplies

Everything you
might find

in a well
stocked hospital
pharmacy

You see
there's a
gap there...

Those medicines
were to treat
water borne
illnesses I expect

In the 1970s
they realised
climate change
would bring
new diseases,

or mutated
forms of
the old ones

and that they could
wipe out
the indigenous
population,

just like
the common cold
brought to the
Aztecs

Some of
the experiments
in the
Time Out
Zones were
to try and forecast
what these
illnesses
might be...

FILM

(To the end of the scene.)

Film flickers... It is the film shot by the women secretly at night in the Time Out Zone, of the Experiments on women prisoners.

Women crammed together in a tank of filthy water. Shot in extreme close up... parts of bodies. As they become more submerged, Images of Panic...

HALL: ... and to
develop
the drugs

to target
them

He points.

Further back
there is hospital
machinery and
equipment.

In those large
steel vats are

supplies of
fresh water,

and water
purifying agents

And there's
crates and crates of
non-perishable
food...

It goes
on and on

beyond what
you can see

and that's
the same
for Every Zone

SHEANN: So...?

HALL: Well even
with planning
it would not
be possible
to make
preparations
for an entire
population

they had
to make
hard choices

This store
room is
set aside
for an
Elite

of Zone 6

It's the
same with
every Zone

SHEANN: An Elite?

HALL: The rich of course
the powerful,
Heads of State,
their bureaucrats
and civil servants,
the intelligentsia,
the beautiful,
the well-connected,

and to insure their survival –
a cross section of doctors...
IT specialists... plumbers...

I am on their list

but

you are
not
of course

nor Cordelia.

SHEANN: Not very...
Christian then

HALL: No.

SHEANN: *(She laughs. She is wild.)*
So this
is the
horror is
it?
She laughs.

FILM

We travel into smaller and darker rooms.

Not the light
shone into
my eyes
so bright

it razored
out my
cornea,

not the
sweet green
water

we were
encouraged
to drink that
made our
bellies explode ,

not the
pill in a
milky drink

that left
us willing
to co-operate

when they
injected our
joints.
while
you sat
in your
office
and collected data
to ensure
the survival

of your
human race

These things
don't shock
you

These are
not horrors!

<u>FILM</u>

Still travelling into dark, empty rooms.

For the first time with the film there is a faint sound, a baby crying.

SHEANN: But
a pile of
tinned peas
cookers and
cars,

put on
one side
for the usual
lucky bleeders.

That shocks you?

Offends you?

Does it?

Answer me!

ANSWER ME!

Silence.

HALL: You see
it struck
me that
it simply
wasn't fair.

Pause.

SHEANN: Where's my
baby?

John Hall

There hasn't
been a day
of my life
I haven't
looked into
the black
shrinking water
hoping to
see her
sweet smile

What happened
to my
baby?

to all
the lost
babies?

Where were they taken?

Mm?

What did
you do

to our
babies?

FILM

The travelling stops… we see the corner of a child's cot. The torch shakes very faintly.

WOMAN 1: Oh my
God.

WOMAN 2: No

WOMAN 3: **Keep filming**

Film flickers to black.

<u>SOUND</u>

In the distance, an insurgent crowd getting closer.

SCENE 25

Pitch blackness.

<u>SOUND</u>

The rioting crowds are deafening, more gunshots, screams and angry cries. The tunnels and store room are being violently stormed.

SHEANN: *(Sweating, whispering.)*

I will never

stop searching

You swam
in
the past

of my

womb.

You were
born

from 40
fathers

and I
thank each
one

born
sticky and
frowning

changing everything
with your
first
breath

I was
your world

But I
saw the
mighty sea

and a

forever sky

reflected in
your eyes

And when
I
held you

you smelt

of treeroots
and rain

I didn't
realise that
love could
be so
sharp

Nobody told
me

that I
would feel
the universe
in your
heartbeat

And
I didn't
understand
a new born babe
could dream

What of?

Before?

And
Beyond?

When you
opened your
eyes

Your tiny
fingers

gripped mine

And they

were so fierce

I will
never stop
searching

SOUND

A voice... "he's in there. He's in there with one of his whores."

a stampede of feet. More screams and cries.

Then...

Perfect silence.

FILM

*Film flickers into a long shot. Night. A Riverbank full of women.
They sit quietly facing the camera.*

A sudden beam of light finds HALL brutally lynched by the crowd...
his shirt pulled over his head.

He swings from the rafters.

A second small beam as from a torch...

... finds SHEANN... a little way off. She too has been lynched. Clothes
pulled over her head.

We see them in an instant only – then...

Blackness.

SCENE 26

CORDELIA's house. Morning. Sunshine.

A young woman is singing, sweet and cheerful... casually as if whilst busy.

CORDELIA is still lying down but covered now in a soft, clean, blanket.

She opens her eyes.

It is a warm English afternoon. As if Spring.

A young girl (perhaps 13) appears, who looks exactly like SHEANN but
her face is not disfigured.

She wears a simple, clean, white dress and looks like a nurse or a nun.

EGASHA: *(Sounding nothing like SHEANN.)*

> Oh...
> you're awake
> at last

> *CORDELIA is entranced, mystified.*

CORDELIA: Sheann...

> Your face
> is healed

EGASHA: You look
> shit.

217

Sorry

I'm not
Sheann

CORDELIA: Not
    Sheann?

EGASHA: I'm
    Egasha

    Can you
    sit up?

    You must
    drink

    but tiny
    sips.

    You
    smell
    like
    a dead
    goat but
    never mind.

She takes out what might be a very old vacuum flask, and puts it to CORDELIA's mouth. CORDELIA tries to sip.

CORDELIA: If you're
    not Sheann
    Who are you?
    Why are you
    here?

    And where
    is she?

EGASHA: I don't
    know

    You were
    completely

on your
own.

I'm from
the other
side of
the river

CORDELIA: From
    where?

EGASHA: I mean
    I know
    your house,

    I watched
    it being
    built

    when I
    was little

    The whole
    river bank
    was just
    mud hills

    and sticks

    and you
    built your
    beautiful
    house

    over the
    river,
    on its
    glass stilts

    I thought
    it was
    a magic
    castle

CORDELIA: It's falling
    down

EGASHA: Yes

CORDELIA: *(Softly.)*
    Disappearing
    into the boiling
    dust

EGASHA: Will you
    build another
    one?

CORDELIA: *(She thinks.)*
    No

    It was
    built
    out of
    skin and
    blood
    and bone

    I want
    the wretched
    place
    gone.

    I want
    it gone
    forever

EGASHA: Where
    will you
    live next?

CORDELIA: I don't know

EGASHA: If there was
    still a river
    you could
    build a boat

Pause.

CORDELIA: Were
    you
    with the
    women

EGASHA: Yes.

CORDELIA: You left.

EGASHA: We had to
    when the
    river dried
    up
    so we
    didn't get
    sick

CORDELIA: Where did
    you go?

EGASHA: Well we
    travelled for
    weeks
    p'raps months

    Up to
    the hills

CORDELIA: How did
    you get
    there?

EGASHA: We walked

CORDELIA: How did
    you live?

EGASHA: Very quietly.
    Very secretly.

    We planted
    seeds

We grew
our own
food

We learnt
how to make
potions

so that we
could help
people when
they were
sick or
injured

that was
my favourite
bit

We made
shelters

and sometimes
our clothes

I hate
that
I hate
sewing

We worked
hard by
the sun

and rested
at night
when it
was dark

And sometimes
we danced
and sang

And sometimes
we told stories

I don't like
stories with
an ending

CORDELIA: How are
    you here
    now?

EGASHA: We came
    back

CORDELIA: Why?

EGASHA: To help
    and because
    it was our
    home

CORDELIA: And have
    you looked
    after me
    all this
    time?

EGASHA: Me and
    others like
    me,

    but
    I was
    the best.

CORDELIA: How old
    are you?

EGASHA: I'm 13.

CORDELIA: But
    a lot of

The River Women
were old.

old women.

EGASHA: After The
Storms

many many
years ago,
before I
think, you
built your
house,

they found
me

a tiny baby

barely alive
on the
river bank,

they took
me,

cared for
me

raised me,

and they
called me
Egasha which means

Lost.

FILM

*Short excerpts play back... perhaps layered with other small bits of
film never seen of The River Women and EGASHA's secret life.*

As it does, the building fills with the women, ... children and men...

Until the film finally rests on the image of the babe on the river bank.

WWW.OBERONBOOKS.COM

www.ingramcontent.com/pod-product-compliance
Ingram Content Group UK Ltd.
Pitfield, Milton Keynes, MK11 3LW, UK
UKHW020739280225
455688UK00013B/733